**WORLD
HISTORY SERIES** ■ ■ ■

The Salem
Witch Trials

Titles in the World History Series

The Age of Augustus
The Age of Exploration
The Age of Feudalism
The Age of Napoleon
The Age of Pericles
The Alamo
America in the 1960s
The American Frontier
The American Revolution
Ancient Greece
The Ancient Near East
Architecture
Aztec Civilization
The Battle of the
    Little Bighorn
The Black Death
The Byzantine Empire
Caesar's Conquest of Gaul
The California Gold Rush
The Chinese Cultural
    Revolution
The Civil Rights Movement
The Collapse of the
    Roman Republic
The Conquest of Mexico
The Crimean War
The Crusades
The Cuban Missile Crisis
The Cuban Revolution
The Early Middle Ages
Egypt of the Pharaohs
Elizabethan England
The End of the Cold War
The Enlightenment
The French and Indian War
The French Revolution
The Glorious Revolution
The Great Depression
Greek and Roman
    Mythology
Greek and Roman Science
Greek and Roman Sport

Greek and Roman Theater
The History of Rock and Roll
The History of Slavery
Hitler's Reich
The Hundred Years' War
The Industrial Revolution
The Inquisition
The Italian Renaissance
The Late Middle Ages
The Lewis and Clark
    Expedition
The Mexican-American War
The Mexican Revolution
The Mexican War of
    Independence
Modern Japan
The Mongol Empire
The Persian Empire
Prohibition
The Punic Wars
The Reformation
The Relocation of the
    North American Indian
The Renaissance
The Roaring Twenties
The Roman Empire
The Roman Republic
Roosevelt and the New Deal
The Russian Revolution
Russia of the Tsars
The Salem Witch Trials
The Scientific Revolution
The Spread of Islam
The Stone Age
The Titanic
Traditional Africa
Traditional Japan
The Travels of Marco Polo
Twentieth Century Science
The Wars of the Roses
The Watts Riot
Women's Suffrage

WORLD HISTORY SERIES ■ ■ ■

The Salem Witch Trials

by Stuart A. Kallen

Lucent Books, P.O. Box 289011, San Diego, CA 92198-9011

Library of Congress Cataloging-in-Publication Data

Kallen, Stuart A., 1955–
    The Salem witch trials / by Stuart A. Kallen.
       p. cm.—(The world history series)
    Includes bibliographical references (p.   ) and index.
    Summary: Discusses the Salem witch trials, including
their Puritan background, the accusations made, and the outcome of the social hysteria that produced the situation.
    ISBN 1-56006-544-3   (lib. : alk. paper)
    1. Trials (Witchcraft)—Massachusetts—Salem—Juvenile
literature.   2. Witchcraft—Massachusetts—Salem—
Juvenile literature.   3. Salem (Mass.)—Social conditions—
Juvenile literature.   [1. Witchcraft—Massachusetts—
Salem.   2. Trials (Witchcraft—Massachusetts—Salem.
3. Salem (Mass.)—History—Colonial period, ca. 1600–1775.]
I. Title. II. Series.
KFM2478.8.W5K35   1999
363.744'50288—dc21   98–52010
                                           CIP
                                           AC

Copyright 1999 by Lucent Books, Inc., P.O. Box 289011,
San Diego, California 92198-9011

Printed in the U.S.A.

Contents

Foreword

Each year on the first day of school, nearly every history teacher faces the task of explaining why his or her students should study history. One logical answer to this question is that exploring what happened in our past explains how the things we often take for granted—our customs, ideas, and institutions—came to be. As statesman and historian Winston Churchill put it, "Every nation or group of nations has its own tale to tell. Knowledge of the trials and struggles is necessary to all who would comprehend the problems, perils, challenges, and opportunities which confront us today." Thus, a study of history puts modern ideas and institutions in perspective. For example, though the founders of the United States were talented and creative thinkers, they clearly did not invent the concept of democracy. Instead, they adapted some democratic ideas that had originated in ancient Greece and with which the Romans, the British, and others had experimented. An exploration of these cultures, then, reveals their very real connection to us through institutions that continue to shape our daily lives.

Another reason often given for studying history is the idea that lessons exist in the past from which contemporary societies can benefit and learn. This idea, although controversial, has always been an intriguing one for historians. Those who agree that society can benefit from the past often quote philosopher George Santayana's famous statement, "Those who cannot remember the past are condemned to repeat it." Historians who subscribe to Santayana's philosophy believe that, for example, studying the events that led up to the major world wars or other significant historical events would allow society to chart a different and more favorable course in the future.

Just as difficult as convincing students to realize the importance of studying history is the search for useful and interesting supplementary materials that present historical events in a context that can be easily understood. The volumes in Lucent Books' World History Series attempt to present a broad, balanced, and penetrating view of the march of history. Ancient Egypt's important wars and rulers, for example, are presented against the rich and colorful backdrop of Egyptian religious, social, and cultural developments. The series engages the reader by enhancing historical events with these cultural contexts. For example, in *Ancient Greece,* the text covers the role of women in that society. Slavery is discussed in *The Roman Empire,* as well as how slaves earned their freedom. The numerous and varied aspects of everyday life in these and other societies are explored in each volume of the series. Additionally, the series covers the major political, cultural, and philosophical ideas as the torch of civilization is passed from ancient Mesopotamia and Egypt, through Greece, Rome, Medieval Europe, and other world cultures, to the modern day.

The material in the series is formatted in a thorough, precise, and organized manner. Each volume offers the reader a comprehensive and clearly written overview of an important historical event or period. The topic under discussion is placed in a broad historical context. For example, *The Italian Renaissance* begins with a discussion of the High Middle Ages and the loss of central control that allowed certain Italian cities to develop artistically. The book ends by looking forward to the Reformation and interpreting the societal changes that grew out of the Renaissance. Thus, students are not only involved in an historical era, but also enveloped by the events leading up to that era and the events following it.

One important and unique feature in the World History Series is the primary and secondary source quotations that richly supplement each volume. These quotes are useful in a number of ways. First, they allow students access to sources they would not normally be exposed to because of the difficulty and obscurity of the original source. The quotations range from interesting anecdotes to farsighted cultural perspectives and are drawn from historical witnesses both past and present. Second, the quotes demonstrate how and where historians themselves derive their information on the past as they strive to reach a consensus on historical events. Lastly, all of the quotes are footnoted, familiarizing students with the citation process and allowing them to verify quotes and/or look up the original source if the quote piques their interest.

Finally, the books in the World History Series provide a detailed launching point for further research. Each book contains a bibliography specifically geared toward student research. A second, annotated bibliography introduces students to all the sources the author consulted when compiling the book. A chronology of important dates gives students an overview, at a glance, of the topic covered. Where applicable, a glossary of terms is included.

In short, the series is designed not only to acquaint readers with the basics of history, but also to make them aware that their lives are a part of an ongoing human saga. Perhaps they will then come to the same realization as famed historian Arnold Toynbee. In his monumental work, *A Study of History*, he wrote about becoming aware of history flowing through him in a mighty current, and of his own life "welling like a wave in the flow of this vast tide."

Important Dates in the History of the Salem Witch Trials

1626	1630	1640	1650

1626

Salem Town is founded.

1630

Settlement of Salem Village begins.

1680

George Burroughs is hired as reverend for Salem Village.

1683

Burroughs leaves Salem.

1684

Deodat Lawson replaces Burroughs.

November 1689
Samuel Parris is made preacher of Salem Village.

1692

January

Abigail Williams and Elizabeth Parris begin acting strangely and having fits.

February
Parris's slaves, Tituba and John Indian, bake a "witch cake" with the girls' urine and feed it to a dog. Other girls, including Ann Putnam and Elizabeth Hubbard, begin having fits. They accuse Tituba, Sarah Good, and Sarah Osburn of bewitching them.

March 1–5

The accused witches are examined in the Salem Village meetinghouse by John Hathorne and Jonathan Corwin. The women are sent to prison two days later.

March 6–19

The afflicted girls accuse Martha Corey of bewitching them.

March 19

Deodat Lawson arrives in the village.

March 21

Martha Corey is examined and sent to prison.

March 21–23

Ann Putnam Jr.'s mother, Ann Sr., joins the afflicted. They accuse Rebecca Nurse of witchcraft.

March 24

Nurse and Good's four-year-old daughter, Dorcas, are examined and sent to prison.

April

Accusations and examinations continue. By the end of the month, twenty-three more suspects are in jail, including John and Elizabeth Proctor, Bridget Bishop, Giles Corey, and George Burroughs.

May

Another thirty-nine people are arrested for witchcraft.

1660   1670   1680   1690   1693

May 10

Sarah Osburn dies in jail.

May 14

William Phipps is appointed royal governor of Massachusetts. Increase Mather arrives from England with a new charter.

June 2

Phipps appoints a Court of Oyer and Terminer to try accused witches. Bridget Bishop is tried and sentenced to hang.

June 10

Bishop is hanged on Gallows Hill. One of the judges, Nathaniel Saltonstall, resigns. Meanwhile, the accusations spread to the villages of Ipswich, Andover, and Gloucester.

June 30

Five more accused witches, including Rebecca Nurse, Elizabeth Howe, and Sarah Good, are tried and convicted.

July 19

Five condemned women are hanged on Gallows Hill.

August 5

The trials continue, and six people are sentenced to die by hanging.

August 19

The second round of hangings kills five convicted witches. Elizabeth Proctor is spared because she is pregnant.

September 9

Six more are tried and sentenced to death.

September 16

Giles Corey is sentenced to be pressed to death, He dies September 19.

September 17

Nine more are sentenced to death.

September 22

Eight of the accused are hanged in the last round of executions.

October

A backlash against the trials and hangings increases.

October 12

Phipps forbids further imprisonment for witchcraft.

October 29

Phipps dissolves the Court of Oyer and Terminer.

1693

January 3

A special court is formed to try the last of the accused witches. Only three are found guilty. Phipps grants them reprieves.

May

Upon payment of their prison fees, Phipps orders the release of the remaining accused witches.

From Goddess to Evil

The Salem witch hysteria that condemned nineteen innocent people to die was not unique in history. In Europe, beginning in the twelfth century, and continuing for more than six hundred years, women, men—and even children—had been imprisoned, tortured, and executed for alleged witchcraft. During the witch-hunts of the fifteenth, sixteenth, and seventeenth centuries, hundreds of thousands of women were put to death for supposedly practicing witchcraft.

Goddess Worship

The roots of what is called witchcraft lie in the earliest days of human existence—a time when women were worshiped for their magical life-giving powers. Archaeologists have found ancient sculptures of women carved from stone, bone, and the ivory tusks of woolly mammoths. These statues, called "Venus figurines," have been found over a wide area of Europe, from France to Siberia, in Austria and the Balkan states. Similar statues have been found in Africa and the Middle East.

Scholars have theorized that the Venuses were the first works of religious art. The noted mythologist Joseph Campbell explains:

> There can be no doubt that in the very earliest ages of human history the magical force and wonder of the female was no less a marvel than the universe itself; and this gave women a prodigious power, which it has been one of the chief concerns of the masculine part of the population to break, control, and employ to its own ends.[1]

As civilizations grew in the area now known as the Mideast, the goddess was the main object of worship. In Canaan, Babylon, and Sumeria, the goddess was given many names—Ishtar, Astarte, and Inanna. In these agriculturally based civilizations, the goddess was considered the source of all life, death, creation, and reincarnation.

But the goddess-worshiping cultures did not last. In about 4000 B.C., warring tribes of hunters began to invade the area—the Semites from the south and Hellenic and Aryan tribes from Europe and Russia. These intruders had a belief system based on bravery and conquest. They invaded the farm cultures and tried to banish goddess worship. In the goddess's place they installed warlike male gods. Before long the goddess came to be portrayed as evil. In dozens of myths from this time, the goddess became a demon who was destroyed in dramatic battles above the clouds. These images of evil were later attached to witches, who, centuries later, kept goddess worship alive.

As civilization progressed, and Europe became more populated, each area developed its own goddess myths. In Germany, the goddess Holda was believed to rule over farming, marriage, childbirth, and home. Holda was thought to be more active in winter when she rode through the sky with her female warriors called Valkyries. Holda was benign, but when angered she turned into the stereotypical witch: an ugly old hag with buckteeth and a long, pointy nose.

Demonizing Witches

Ancient tales that demonized goddesses changed attitudes toward powerful men and women who were often thought of as sorcer-

ers or witches. Like the goddesses, sorcerers were believed to be able to use their magic powers for good *and* evil, light *and* dark. According to the book *Witches and Witchcraft:*

> Because of this dual capacity for good and evil, every practitioner of magic and sorcery, no matter how closely attached to a tribe or family, was regarded with grave uneasiness. The folktales of the [ancient] peoples reflect a deep-seated fear of the sorcerer's presumed mastery over the most frightful powers of nature. They show that long before people made the connection between human magic and the powers of Satan, they believed that sorcerers could command the storm clouds, cause harvests to wither and die, unleash famine, and bring down pestilence. No one was considered immune to the sorcerer's spell. An angry magician could influence the process of life itself, making men impotent and inducing entire herds of cattle to abort their calves.[2]

A man visits a witch as she sits before her boiling cauldron. Witches and sorcerers were thought to have the power to conjure both good and evil spells.

These beliefs were taken very seriously by peasants and government officials. European people in all walks of life believed in sorcerers called *tempestarii*, who could conjure up violent storms, steal crops, and load them on their cloud ships to be carried off to a fabled country called Magnonia.

The Church's Power and the *Witches' Hammer*

By the ninth century, the Christian church was the all-powerful ruler of continental Europe. According to the church, demons used magic and sorcery to seduce innocent people into worshiping evil. Fortune-tellers, folk healers, witches, wizards, and sorcerers were lumped together as the Devil's demons and were believed to fly through the night, seduce innocent people, and sometimes transform themselves into animals. By the tenth century, witchcraft meant entering into a formal covenant with the Devil.

Ignorance, mistrust, and fear of witches came to a head in 1485, when Pope Innocent VII declared that witchcraft was a reality rather than a myth. To deny Innocent's words was heresy, punishable by death. Adding fuel to the fire was a book entitled *Malleus Maleficarum*, or *Witches' Hammer*, written in 1486 by two Germans—Heinrich Kramer and Jakob Sprenger. The 250,000-word *Witches' Hammer* detailed everything known or imagined about witches. It combined folk beliefs about sorcery with church

Potions and Charms

Records show that sorcerers brewed potions for love and offered charms and amulets to protect against injury and death. They also used magical skills to cure the sick. According to *Witches and Witchcraft,* by the editors of Time-Life Books:

> One Anglo-Saxon recipe for the treatment of warts called for "the water [urine] of a dog and the blood of a mouse" to be mixed together and smeared on the afflicted part. Sorcerers among these same people concocted a "pleasant drink against insanity" from catnip, wormwood, lupine, radish, fennel, cat's mint, enchanter's nightshade, and a number of other herbs all steeped in strong ale. This formula, dating from the Christian era, included a dose of that religion. "Sing twelve Masses over the drink, and let the patient drink it. He will soon be better," advised the sorcerer.

The worst punishment for being a witch was death, often by being burned at the stake. Here three women are consumed by flames as a demon escapes from the mouth of one of the condemned.

doctrine on demon worship. *Witches' Hammer* contained guidelines for holding trials, obtaining confessions, and examining witnesses. Included were suggestions for the most effective types of torture. The book also claimed that the entire female gender was evil, vain, mean-spirited, and weak. "What else is a woman but a foe to friendship," the writers asked, "an inescapable punishment, a necessary evil, a natural temptation?"[3] The authors said it was no wonder that the Devil sought them out. This turned the focus of witchhunters exclusively to women. (Thousands of men, called wizards, would die in the witch-hunts, but most of the victims were women.)

By the mid-1700s, a few people were brave enough to take a stand against mass murder of alleged witches. The Age of Enlightenment had dawned. Science, education, and reason began to push witch-hunting into history. The last convicted witches in England died in 1682. They were three old women who wearily climbed the gallow's steps at Exeter. The last witch was burned alive in France in 1745, and in Germany in 1775.

No one knows exactly how many women died during the witch-hunting insanity in Europe. Guesses range from two hundred thousand to 2 million. Whatever the number, a huge percentage of women were killed in the name of good. Although witch-hunting was officially over by the 1800s, fear and mistrust of witches continued for centuries.

1 Puritan Life in Salem

Witch-hunts raged across Europe for centuries. The superstitions and fears that caused the persecution crossed into the New World with the English settlers. In the winter of 1692, a wave of witch hysteria engulfed the settlement of Salem Village in Massachusetts Bay Colony. Before it ended, nineteen people were hanged and more than a hundred languished in prison for months, hungry, thirsty, and chained to the walls. These people had their estates and possessions confiscated by the sheriff, their cattle killed, and their children left to fend for themselves. Fallout from the witch madness came to touch almost everybody in New England.

The arrest, imprisonment, torture, and murder of the innocents began in an unlikely way, with the word of two young girls, ages nine and eleven, one a reverend's daughter, the other his niece. The youngsters started accusing people of witchcraft, falling into fits and convulsions as they did so, screaming blasphemies and writhing on the ground. This behavior induced the village's leaders—clergymen, sheriffs, and politicians—to round up dozens of people and put them on trial.

This bizarre chapter in American history may be difficult to understand from a modern perspective. But in seventeenth-century New England there was nothing unusual about fits involving bodily contortions and meaningless babble. This group of English settlers—known as Puritans—had very few outlets for their emotions, and the repressive nature of their society only allowed spirited outburst in the context of deep religious rapture—or religious terror. To the Puritans, witches, demons, and evil spirits were as real as the rocky soil from which they scratched their living.

Salem Village

Salem Village is today the town of Danvers, Massachusetts. At first Salem Village had no formal name. It was referred to as Salem Farms, and the inhabitants were simply called "the Farmers." Salem Village was part of Salem Town, but the two places were separated by distance, class, and style. Salem Town was a prosperous port with fine merchants' houses, well-stocked shops, and large municipal buildings. By contrast, Salem Village consisted of widely scattered farms surrounded by dense forest. Most of the inhabitants were poor and lived a hard life. The official population of Salem Village was 550 in about ninety households. Slaves, servants, and the

The Founding of Salem

In the Bible, Salem is another name for the holy city of Jerusalem. But for all the biblical references in its name, Salem, Massachusetts, began as a money-making venture. The site of Salem Town was selected by Roger Conant in 1626 because of its fine natural harbor on the Atlantic Ocean and its network of rivers that provided access to the interior. The town began as a fishing station and trading post that depended on trade with Europe and the West Indies.

A tide of Puritan immigration started in 1630 and brought prosperity to Salem. The town soon outgrew the narrow neck of land where it was located, and the thin soil there lacked the fertility needed to feed the growing population. In response to these pressures, townsmen gave grants of up to three hundred acres to businessmen to settle the hinterlands as far west as Ipswich, seven miles away.

Prosperous from the start, by 1660, Salem Town entered an era of economic expansion based on trade. Before long, the expansion led to an urban pattern of life far different from that of Salem Village. Salem Town's importance was officially recognized in 1683 when it was designated, along with Boston, as a "port of entry." That meant that all imports and exports to the colony had to pass through Boston or Salem Town. This put the town at the center of trade with London, England. Goods such as cod, mackerel, fur, horses, grain, beef, pork, and ship masts were exported from Salem. Tobacco, rum, sugar, cloth, and other products were imported through the town. People who lived in Salem Town lived rich and luxurious lives by New England standards.

homeless were uncounted, so the real number of residents was greater.

Residents of Salem Village rarely went to Salem Town unless they had to, as it was a three-hour walk in each direction and required crossing several large rivers and inlets. Before the village church was built, though, residents were forced to walk to

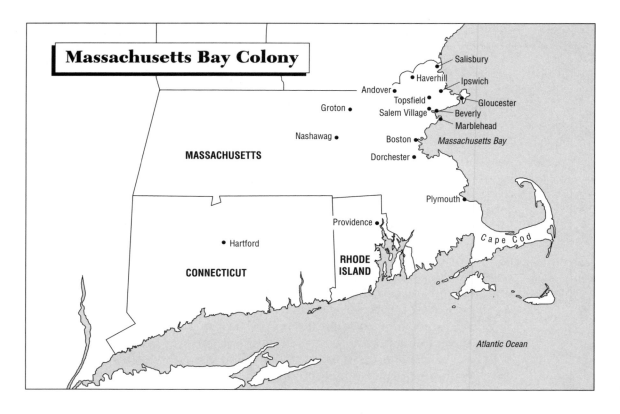

Massachusetts Bay Colony

Salem Town every Sunday to attend church. (On November 11, 1672, the men of Salem Village laid plans for their own meetinghouse and hired a preacher so the long walk each week was eventually eliminated.)

The parsonage (home of the parson) stood at the center of Salem Village, between a tavern and a training ground for local militiamen. Opposite the tavern was a lookout, fortified against Indian raids. (Although Salem Village had never been attacked, there were constant fears that it would be.) A few hundred feet down the road stood a meetinghouse, which would become the site of the witch examinations. Outside of town there were houses belonging to artisans such as potters, shoemakers, cabinetmakers, blacksmiths, and the like.

There were no other buildings besides farmhouses. The village was surrounded by the tall trees of the uncharted wilderness.

Throughout most of its early existence Salem Village failed repeatedly to gain independence from Salem Town. The town not only collected taxes from the village but determined the prices that it would pay for farm products purchased from the villagers. The town also appointed the village's constable and determined land grants and road routes. The tensions of this situation caused a high level of bickering and disorganization within the village.

For more than a century, the conflict between the townsmen and the farmers produced scores of petitions, resolutions, and protests by both sides. Salem Village remained under the control of Salem Town until 1752.

Puritan Religion

Puritans, also called Congregationalists, were part of the Church of England, which had broken away from the Roman Catholic Church in the sixteenth century. They wanted to "purify" their national church by eliminating what they saw as Catholic influence.

In the seventeenth century, the Puritans migrated to the New World, where they founded the holy Commonwealth in New England. They encouraged direct personal religious experience, strict moral conduct, and simple worship services. The Puritans brought strong religious beliefs to all colonies north of Virginia, but New England was their stronghold.

Puritans believed in the absolute sovereignty of God and the total sinfulness of man. They thought that humans were completely dependent on divine grace for salvation, and they insisted that they had the duty to direct national affairs according to God's will. They formed a union of church and state—a system known as theocracy—to control most activities. Although Puritans did not actively try to convert others to their religion, they expected the many non-Puritan servants and craftsmen (mostly Catholics or Anglicans who emigrated from Ireland and England) to worship at Puritan meetinghouses no matter what their beliefs.

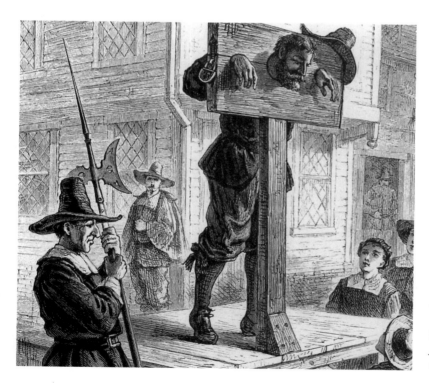

Being locked in wooden stocks was one of the humiliating punishments people endured for breaking Puritan laws and codes.

Those who were deemed sinners were severely punished. The wretches who broke the rules were usually servants or the poor. The punishments were meant to humiliate as well as cause pain. Sinners might be locked in wooden stocks so that they could not move as rotten eggs were thrown at them. They were made to stand in public markets with notes describing their offenses stuck on their foreheads. And they were publicly whipped.

Old court records list the petty crimes for which people were punished. According to Frances Hill's book *A Delusion of Satan:*

> Page after page lists crimes such as fornication, "railing and scolding," stealing food, "unseemly practices" on the part of a young woman "betwixt her and another maid," breaking off an engagement, "unseemly speeches against the rule of the Church," sleeping during a service and "striking him who awakened him." Almost no offense against the Puritans' rigid code of belief and behavior was too trivial for punishment.[4]

Many crimes revolved around the strict code Puritans had about observing the Sunday Sabbath. For example, in the winter of 1647 a man fell into a pool of water late on Saturday night. He could not dry his only suit of clothes by Sunday morning, so he stayed in bed to keep warm. He was convicted of "slothfulness" and whipped for not attending church. On a Sunday in 1656, a Boston man kissed his wife in public after returning from three years at sea. He was sentenced to two hours in the stocks for "lewd and unseemly" behavior.

Puritans had no tolerance for other religions. They especially hated Quakers, whom they whipped, tortured, and sometimes hanged for their beliefs.

Puritan Church Services

The only break in work for the Puritans came on Sunday mornings when all attended church. The Puritan Sabbath was strictly observed from sunup to sundown. Services lasted three hours in the morning and two hours in the afternoon. The rest of the day was spent in religious reading, prayer recitation, and at-home contemplation. Any activities not purely religious were regarded as sinful.

Observance of the Sabbath was mandated by law. In addition to Sunday services, Thursdays were "lecture days," when the population was expected to attend a midweek sermon. Even church services were seen as offering opportunities for sin. Services took place in plain wooden meetinghouses with no decorations. Psalms were sung in monotone to prevent any possible pleasure—considered sinful—in singing. At services, a person called the "tithing man" walked up and down the aisles poking those who fell asleep or fidgeted during the long sermons. To ensure that there was no flirting, men sat on the west side of the aisle, women on the east. Children and servants were seated in galleries built along the walls.

The Puritans were as class-conscious as their relatives back in England. Seating during church services was determined by one's wealth. The few richest citizens —"Lords," "Sirs," and "Ladies"—sat in the front row. The next wealthiest were called "Mr." and "Mrs." and sat farther back. Ordinary folk were deemed "Goodman" and "Goodwife" (the latter sometimes shortened simply to "Goody"); these people sat in the back of the meetinghouse.

Church services were held in plain wooden meetinghouses that were cold and dark during the winter months and infested with mosquitoes and other pests in the summer.

There was no heating in the meeting-houses. On the coldest days, the windows stayed shuttered and pastors read sermons by candlelight. The congregation was allowed to bring blankets and pans filled with hot coals or hot bricks to warm the feet. Well-behaved dogs could also be used for warmth. On the coldest days, services were held in taverns that were heated by a fireplace. As for the summer months, the village meetinghouse was located on the edge of a swamp, with mosquitoes, ticks, and flies adding to the discomfort.

The Puritan Household

During the long, cold, dark Massachusetts winters, the warm hearth was the centerpiece of family life. The hearth was used for cooking all food as well as providing heat for the household. On frigid January mornings, children would awaken to the sound of their father or mother stoking the hearth and pumping the bellows to breathe new life into the fire. Inside, homes were dark. Windows had tiny panes of dark glass that let in little light. In the middle of winter, candles were needed all day.

After breakfast, girls started on chores, helping their mothers sew, spin wool, cook, clean, and wash. There was always plenty of work, since families had to make their own bread, butter, cider, ale, clothes, candles, and almost everything else they used.

Puritan cooks had no problem finding ingredients for the dishes they prepared. Venison and other game came from the forest, and there was plenty of fish in the rivers. They raised their own meat and poultry and planted vegetable

Puritans and Ale

It may seem strange that deeply religious Puritans freely drank ale. But they came from England, where there was an ancient tradition of drinking ale or beer. In Europe up until the fifteenth century, beer was mainly brewed by monks and given away at churches to increase attendance. As a matter of fact, beer is mentioned in the Bible. Three of the rabbis who wrote the Old Testament (the Hebrew Bible) were brewers, as was King David.

There was a reason behind the popularity of beer, besides the euphoric effects. Most rivers, lakes, and streams were so polluted in Europe that to drink from them would be a death sentence. Beer, because it is boiled when it is brewed, kills harmful bacteria and microbes in the water.

Everyone drank beer or alcoholic cider with their meals. Puritans brewed their own beer and served a watered-down style of ale to children. Alcohol was not forbidden, but drunkenness was.

Drinking alcohol was not forbidden by the Puritans.

gardens. Spices imported from the West Indies and herbs grown at home flavored traditional recipes brought from England, such as salmon in ale. Cooks mixed sweet sauces with meat in dishes such as venison in maple syrup and apple-pork pie.

At midday the Puritans ate lunch—called dinner—and in the evening they ate

Puritans did not allow harsh conditions to keep them from going to worship services.

supper. After the dishes were cleared away, a typical family would read from scriptures and sing psalms. Then it was off to bed in a rope hammock, a stuffed mattress, or simply a pile of straw strewn on the floor.

If the weather permitted, Puritans might walk a few hundred yards to visit their next-door neighbor. But given the harsh climate, rough terrain, and lack of decent roads, visits were few. And visits for mere pleasure were regarded as dubious activities, bordering on sinful. In fact, Puritans regarded any activities besides work and prayer as sinful distractions.

Puritan Children

Strict rules of conduct applied to Puritan children as well as to adults. There was little play or amusement, few toys or dolls. Nathaniel Hawthorne describes seventeenth-century Puritan children's play in his novel *The Scarlet Letter:*

[Children played] in such grim fashion as the Puritanic nature would permit; playing at going to church, perchance; or at scourging Quakers; or in taking scalps in a sham-fight with the Indians; or scaring one another with freaks of imitative witchcraft.[5]

Although *The Scarlet Letter* is a work of fiction, it accurately describes Puritan life. Hawthorne lived in Salem in the nineteenth century. One of his ancestors, in fact, was a leading magistrate in the Salem witch trials.

Childhood ended at an early age. By the time they were six or seven, children were expected to work at all household chores. One Boston clergyman wrote in his diary that he expected his five- and six-year-old daughters to help upholster chairs and make curtains.

The only books in Puritan households were religious in theme. Some included graphic accounts by clergymen of supernatural incidents involving witches, spirits, and demons. They were sensationalized

The Mather Family

The oddly named Cotton Mather was a member of a family that held tremendous influence over the shape and direction of Puritanism in Massachusetts for three generations. Cotton's grandfather Richard (1596–1669) was expelled from the Church of England for criticizing Anglican worship ceremonies. He moved to the Massachusetts Bay Colony, where he was immediately recognized as a leader of the Puritan church. He served as a minister in Dorchester for thirty-three years.

Richard's son Increase Mather (1639–1723) was a minister of Boston's Second Congregational Church. There he shaped the lives and values of second-generation New England Puritans through his authorship of 130 books and pamphlets. (A word about the names: In those days it was common to give children bizarre-sounding names. One family's children, for example, were named Truegrace, Reform, Hopedfor, More Mercy, and Restore.) Increase Mather believed in witches but cautioned against the unproved accusations at the Salem witch trials and helped end the executions. Increase was president of Harvard from 1685 to 1701.

Cotton Mather (1663–1728), son of Increase, was an ordained minister in his father's church. Of all the Puritans, Cotton was the most prolific writer. During his forty-three years as preacher and pastor he wrote 450 books on a variety of topics. Although Cotton fanned the flames of the Salem witch hysteria, he later criticized the executions.

Interested in the scientific developments of his time, Cotton defended the smallpox vaccination long before it was proved safe. He was one of the few Americans named a fellow of the prestigious Royal Society in London.

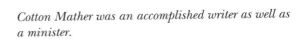

Cotton Mather was an accomplished writer as well as a minister.

(intended to arouse intense emotional reaction) and meant to counter skepticism and disbelief at such occurrences. Few children read anything but the Bible, a catechism (instruction on religious beliefs), a hymnbook, or the almanac.

Most girls did not know how to read. There were few schools for girls in seventeenth-century New England, and none at all in Salem Village. Young women of that time had nothing at all to feed their imaginations. There were no fairy tales or stories, no art, theater, or classical music. Boys were allowed to enjoy hunting, trapping, fishing, carpentry, and crafts, but girls were not allowed to participate in such activities.

The lives of children were filled, as were those of adults, with anxiety and fear. There was a constant danger of Indian attacks, serious illness, and death. Terror and shame were instilled in even the youngest. Children were forced to repress all feelings of joy, rebelliousness, and anger. To exhibit anything but submissive behavior was to risk being branded as evil. Just like adults, small children were told that they were in danger of hellfire. Thoughtful children agonized over every move, fearful that they might sin by accident. Their fears were not eased by the leading Boston minister Cotton Mather, who, in the preface of a children's book, thundered:

Do you dare to run up and down upon the Lord's day! Or do you keep in to read your book! They which lie, must go to their father the devil, into everlasting burning; they which never pray, God will pour out his wrath upon them; and when they beg and pray in hell fire, God will not forgive them, but there [they] must lie forever. Are you willing to go to hell to be burnt with the devil and his angels? . . . Oh, hell is a terrible place, that's worse a thousand times than whipping.[6]

Given the constant thundering about Satan, sin, and spells by adult Puritans, it is not surprising that a sensitive young child might be subject to fits and weeping and hysterical talk about witchcraft. What is surprising is how seriously these accusations were taken and how an entire colony of people, from poor farmers to the governor himself, would be whipped into hysteria by two little girls who claimed to see Satan behind almost every door.

Chapter

2 Madness Comes to Salem

While people in Europe were falsely accusing and killing thousands of women for witchcraft, the madness was less intense in New England. As Massachusetts governor Thomas Hutchinson pointed out in 1750, "more [suspected witches were] put to death in a single county in England, in a short space of time, than have suffered in all New England from the first settlement to the present time."[7]

In Europe, fear of witches and witchcraft smoldered—and often burned out of control—over the course of several centuries. By that measure, witch hysteria came to Salem Village rather late. But when it did finally arrive, it flamed with a vengeance, leaving a trail of broken lives—wounded, dead, and innocent—behind.

There were few cases of seventeenth-century New England witch hangings before the Salem witch trials. But the few there were helps throw light on the Salem trials, which occurred later in the century.

New England's First Witch Trials

The earliest recorded witchcraft case in North America is that of Anne Hibbins, who was said to be the sister of former Massachusetts governor Richard Belling-

ham. Hibbins's husband, who died in 1654, was an important merchant. Anne herself was reportedly a quarrelsome woman—enough so that she was officially censured in church for it. One day Hibbins came upon two neighbors talking, and said she knew the neighbors were talking about her. Hibbins then reconstructed the conversation with enough accuracy to convince the neighbors she was possessed of supernatural powers.

Hibbins was brought to trial in 1655, and a jury found her guilty. But the presiding judges refused to accept the verdict, which threw the case into a higher court. Again Hibbins was found guilty, and the governor of the colony sentenced her to death. She was executed in 1656. But not everyone was convinced of her guilt. A surviving letter by a Reverend John Norton, who knew Hibbins, states that

> [Hibbins] was hanged for a witch only for having more wit than her neighbors. . . she having. . . unhappily guessed that two of her persecutors, whom she saw talking in the street, were talking of her,—which cost her life.[8]

Another case took place in Hartford, Connecticut, in 1662. Anne Cole, a highly esteemed and pious woman, was taken with strange fits. Boston minister Increase

A portion of the verdict that in 1656 sentenced Anne Hibbins to death for witchcraft.

Mather wrote about Cole in *An Essay for the Recordings of Illustrious Providences,* published in 1684:

> Very Remarkable was that Providence wherein Ann[e] Cole of Hartford in New-England was concerned. She was and is accounted a person of real Piety and Integrity. Nevertheless, in the Year 1662, then living in her Fathers House (who has likewise been esteemed a godly Man) She was taken with very strange Fits, wherein her Tongue was improved by a Demon to express things which she her self knew nothing of. Sometimes the Discourse would hold for a considerable time. The general purpose of which was, that such and such persons (who were named in the Discourse which passed from her) were consulting how they might carry on mischievous designs against her and several others, mentioning sundry wayes they should take for that end, particularly that they would afflict her Body, spoil her Name, etc.

At that point Anne Cole began babbling incoherently, and then in Dutch, a language "which Ann[e] Cole had not in the least been [familiar with]." Several men who understood Dutch wrote down what Cole was saying. She told the story of "a Woman . . . whose Arms had been strangely pinched in the night." The event was caused by Rebecca Greensmith, "a lewd and ignorant Woman, and then in Prison on suspicion for Witchcraft . . . as active in the mischiefs done and designed." The magistrate was sent for, and Greensmith

> confessed . . . that she and other persons named in this preternatural [supernatural] Discourse, had familiarity with the Devil. . . . She then acknowledged . . . that the Devil first appeared to her in the form of a Deer or Fawn, skipping about her, wherewith she was not much affrighted, and that by degrees he became very familiar, and at last would talk with her. Moreover, she said that the Devil had frequently the carnal knowledge of her Body. . . . Upon this Confession . . . the Woman was Executed; so likewise was her husband, though he did not acknowledge himself guilty. . . . After the suspected Witches were . . . executed . . . Ann[e] Cole was restored to health, and has continued well for many years, approving her self a serious Christian.[9]

As a result of Anne Cole's testimony, Rebecca and Nathaniel Greensmith were hanged in Hartford in January 1663. Before she died, Rebecca Greensmith accused several others of witchcraft, and they were also hanged.

Mather goes on to fill page after page of his essay with "Diabolical Molestations" experienced by New England farmers, including chairs flying through the air; beds dancing; invisible spirits beating people; children barking like dogs; and cheese being ripped from the hands of those eating it.

Another case of witchcraft was recorded in the summer of 1688, when the children of a "sober and pious" mason, John Good-

Suffering from Hysteria

The fits and convulsions of the afflicted girls would today be diagnosed as symptoms of hysteria. Hysteria is a clinical psychological condition whose victims may suffer from amnesia, hallucinations, sleepwalking, and paralysis without apparent cause. Symptoms may also include convulsive movements, distorted postures, and the loss of hearing, sight, and speech. The condition is sometimes caused by extreme anxiety. It is a powerful physical experience that may involve rapid or pounding heartbeat, difficult breathing, sweating, dry mouth, tightness in the chest, sweaty palms, dizziness, weakness, nausea, diarrhea, cramps, insomnia, fatigue, headache, loss of appetite, and other disturbances.

Psychologists who have studied hysterics have noted that often, after hours of howling and convulsions, the patient experiences relaxation and may return to ordinary life until the next fit. But hysterics may be notoriously suggestible—that is, beliefs and memories may be planted that were not present before and are not based on reality. This would explain why Salem women in hysterical fits may have agreed to the suggestions of witchcraft implied by authorities.

Although hysteria most often affects women (gender of all the accusers), it is also found in men, particularly those who have experienced trauma in war. The type of convulsive fits displayed by Abigail Williams and the others were observed in patients in military hospitals during World War II.

The title page of Cotton Mather's Memorable Providences.

win, began having strange fits. As Cotton Mather writes in *Memorable Providences:*

Sometimes [the children] would be Deaf, sometimes Dumb, and sometimes Blind, and often all at once. One while their Tongues would be drawn down their Throats; another-while they would be pull'd out upon their Chins, to a prodigious length. They would have their Mouths opened unto such a Wideness, that their Jaws went out of joint; and anon they would clap together again with a Force like that of a strong Spring-Lock. The same would happen to their Shoulder-Blades, and their Elbows, and Hand-Wrists, and several of their joints. . . . They would make the most pitteous out-cries, that they were cut with Knives, and struck with Blows that they could not bear. . . . Yea and their Heads would be twisted almost round.[10]

These fits started after one of the children quarreled with an Irish washerwoman, Goodwife Glover, who was, according to Mather, "the Daughter of an ignorant and a scandalous old Woman in the Neighborhood; whose miserable Husband. . . complained of her that she was undoubtedly a witch."[11] Glover, who was a hated Roman Catholic, was accused of witchcraft and hanged.

Parson Parris and His Family

Three years after Goodwife Glover was hanged, witch hysteria came to Salem Village. It began in the parsonage of Samuel Parris. Reverend Parris had moved to Salem Village from Boston in 1689 with his wife, three children, and his niece Abigail Williams. Parris also brought with him a Caribbean Indian slave couple from Barbados named Tituba and John Indian.

The appointment of Parris as reverend generated controversy in Salem Village. Townsmen who arranged the ordination voted to give Samuel Parris the parsonage, which was owned by the village. This included a large house, a barn, and two acres of land. The land grant was in direct violation of a law adopted earlier by the village council that said the parsonage would be owned by the residents of the village and would not be transferred to any person. In addition to the house, the reverend was granted an annual salary of sixty-six pounds.

Parris was a man obsessed with his own status and with finding sinfulness everywhere. He believed a strict Puritan theology that made absolutes of good and evil, sin and saintliness, heaven and hell. The pastor's greatest fear was that Satan would

The parsonage of Reverend Samuel Parris. A barn and two acres of land were also part of the property.

Tituba (right), one of the Parris family's slaves, might have been involved in the occult games that led to the first symptoms of hysteria in Salem.

arm his foes to destroy both his family and his church.

Reverend Parris had come to Salem after failing in many endeavors. His father had left him less than he expected of his estate in England. As a young man, Parris left Harvard without obtaining a degree. He failed in business in the West Indies, which forced him to take the job as a small-town pastor in the backwater of Salem Village. Despite his many failures, Parris projected an air of self-importance, which led the pastor to evoke hatred from many townspeople.

Among the children in the Parris family was a nine-year-old girl named Elizabeth, called Betty, who was steeped in her father's rigid beliefs. Elizabeth's best friend was her eleven-year-old cousin Abigail. When the pastor's wife was sick, which was often, the young girls were left in the care of the slave woman Tituba.

The family's relationship with their slaves was probably an uneasy one because it was unusual for New Englanders to own slaves. And because Tituba and John were Caribbean Indians, they were looked upon with deep suspicion, even by the people they lived with. These feelings were probably harbored by Elizabeth and Abigail, even though they depended on Tituba for daily care.

The Parris family was unusual for owning slaves, and also for having only three children. The average Puritan family of the time might have ten or twelve children. What was not unusual was the presence of cousin Abigail in the household. It was common among the Puritans for children to live with families not their own. Historians have speculated that Puritans were so terrified of earthly indulgences that they often removed their own children from their homes so as not to be overly affectionate. There was also a practical reason for Abigail's presence—she was an orphan, another common situation for children in a land where death through accidents,

Conflicts with Native Americans

It would be hard to exaggerate the fear of Native Americans held by the Puritans who inhabited the Massachusetts Bay Colony. When the English first arrived, the Native Americans welcomed them and were responsible for their survival. But the English took the Indians' land, broke treaties, and enslaved or killed them. They also infected them with smallpox, a disease for which the natives had no immunity. This mistreatment resulted in the death of 75 percent of New England's Native Americans in less than fifty years.

By 1675, the Native Americans were enraged and desperate. This unrest led to a countrywide attack called King Philip's War. The war was so named because the Indian that led the attack, Metacomet—chief of the Wampanoag tribe of Plymouth Colony—was called Philip by the English.

Fighting first broke out in June 1675. The conflict spread rapidly across southern New England, involving the colonies of Plymouth, Massachusetts, Connecticut, and Rhode Island. Indian raiding parties burned many towns and killed or captured hundreds of colonists. Several of the young women in Salem Village who accused others of witchcraft in 1692 had been orphaned as a result of Indian attacks. The colonists soon gained the upper hand and imposed even greater destruction upon the Indians, killing thousands. All resistance was finally crushed. Philip himself was trapped and killed in August 1676.

One in ten white settlers was killed in the war, a greater death toll per capita than any other conflict in American history. King Philip's War lasted less than two years, but it was the most destructive Indian war in New England's history.

disease, and other disasters was a greater risk of everyday existence.

In the strict life forced on a pastor's daughter and niece, Elizabeth Parris and Abigail Williams found ways to relieve their boredom. One way, an innocent game by modern standards, was for young girls to try to predict the occupation of their future husband by pouring an egg white into a glass of water. The shape the egg took, such as that of a hammer or a paintbrush, was believed to determine the future husband's occupation.

Historians venture that the girls were helped in their game by Tituba. Others argue that the egg and glass is a traditional English method of divining, so Caribbean-born Tituba would not have known about it. But since the girls were often in Tituba's care, she certainly could have been involved with the "occult experiment."

In either case, this activity was anything but innocent for two Puritan girls in seventeenth-century New England, especially when the egg white surfaced in the shape of a coffin. It is no wonder the frightened girls soon began to display symptoms of hysteria.

The girls' fits and convulsions lasted for months. In March 1692, the details of the hysterics were recorded by Deodat Lawson. (Lawson had been the parson of Salem Village before Parris arrived. He came to Salem when the witch accusations were at their height.) Lawson wrote about the antics of the afflicted girls in an essay with a typically long title of the day, *A Brief and True Narrative Of some Remarkable Passages Relating to sundry Persons Afflicted by Witchcraft, at Salem Village Which happened from the Nineteenth of March, to the Fifth of April, 1692.* According to *A Brief and True Narrative,* Abigail Williams

had a grievous fit; she was at first hurryed with Violence to and fro in the room . . . sometimes makeing as if she would fly, stretching up her arms as high as she could, and crying "Whish, Whish, Whish!" several times. . . . She r[a]n to the Fire, and beg[a]n to throw Fire Brands, about the house; and run

against the Back, as if she would run up the Chimney, and, as they said, she had attempted to go into the Fire in other Fits.[12]

Lawson makes a list of symptoms suffered, writing that the girls'

motions in their Fits are Preternatural, both as to the manner, which is so strange as a well person could not Screw their Body into; and as to the violence also it is preternatural, being much beyond the Ordinary force of the same person in their right mind.[13]

There were other symptoms as well: temporary loss of sight and hearing; loss of memory, so that they could not recall what happened during the fits; a choking sensation in the throat; loss of appetite; and terrifying hallucinations wherein demons tormented them with pinching and biting. Before long, these symptoms spread to other girls in the community.

Public Displays of Affliction

Pastor Parris treated Abigail's and Elizabeth's afflictions by forcing them to fast and pray. He also took them to a series of doctors. For a time the physicians were puzzled, but one of them, Dr. William Griggs, who lived nearby, said, "The evil hand is upon them; the girls were victims of malefic witchcraft."[14] This diagnosis was not unusual in seventeenth-century medicine. The majority of physicians at that time believed in witchcraft and considered it as the cause of many diseases that they did not understand.

Parris at first refused to believe the girls were bewitched, but the neighbors certainly did. People from all over the countryside traveled to the parsonage to see the afflicted girls. The sudden interest was probably pleasing to the girls; they intensified their strange antics. They began to have their fits on street corners. One Sunday they even had an outburst in church. From that day on, and for almost a year, not a Sunday passed when the girls did not have fits in church. No one noticed that they did not take place during sermons or prayer, but only during lulls in the services.

The show put on by the young girls astonished the townsfolk, who were absolutely certain that it was the work of the Devil. Villagers asked the girls who was afflicting them, but they got no answer. Lacking a concrete cause or a ready treatment, the villagers were desperate. Soon Mary Sibley, the aunt of Mary Walcott, one of the afflicted girls, decided to turn to white magic to break the witch's spell.

Fervent prayer was one of the "cures" used to treat those beset by hallucinations and other symptoms of demonic possession.

The Witch Cake

On February 25, 1692, Goodwife Sibley approached Tituba's husband, John Indian, and asked him to prepare a witch cake from a traditional English recipe—flour mixed with the children's urine. The cake was baked in a fire and fed to the family's dog. Sibley believed that the dog was a "familiar" (a messenger assigned to a witch by the Devil) and feeding it the witch cake would help break the spell that was afflicting the children.

One month later, Pastor Parris found out about Sibley's witch cake. He said it was "going to the Devil for help against the Devil."[15] He lectured Sibley privately and then called her out in church before the entire congregation. In tears, Sibley acknowledged her sinfulness, but it was too late. The witch cake had been baked and, as Parris thundered in a long speech,

> the Devil hath been raised among us, and his rage is vehement and terrible; and, when he shall be silenced, the Lord only knows. But now that this our sister should be instrumental to such distress is a great grief to myself . . . and our . . . neighbors.[16]

The Witch's Pets

Every storybook witch has a black cat to help her in her evildoings. But cats were not the only animals thought to be "familiars"—messengers assigned by the Devil to help a witch. Other suspect animals were ferrets, rabbits, blackbirds, owls, crows, toads, and frogs. Cats and other familiars often served as evidence in seventeenth-century witch trials.

Cat lovers were especially vulnerable because of long-standing superstitions about felines. Cats were worshiped in ancient Egypt, where anyone who killed a cat was subject to the death penalty. The Roman goddess Diana was said to assume a cat form, and the Norse goddess Freya had a chariot pulled by cats. With the advent of Christianity in Europe, the church taught that formerly sacred animals were minor demons. Church doctrine was developed to see the shadow of Satan in anyone who had a strong relationship with an animal.

With the coming of the witch trials, cats were said to have performed magical services for accused witches. One cat was said to have filled up his mistress's pasture with sheep and brought her suitors. The cat was supposedly rewarded one drop of blood for every service performed.

During the mass killings of women accused of witchcraft in Europe, thousands of cats were also killed. This behavior resulted in a huge rise in the disease-spreading rat population, which some historians believe led to the Black Plague in the fourteenth century.

A witch and her black cat, one of the animals considered by Puritans to be messengers of the Devil.

In spite of Parris's denunciation, people in Salem Village believed the cake had worked its magic by allowing the girls to name their tormentors. On February 29, Williams and Parris accused Tituba, along with two old women whom no one in the village seemed to like: Sarah Good and Sarah Osburn.

It was no mystery why Good and Osburn were singled out. They were middle-aged outcasts—awkward, ill-mannered, and despised by the villagers. Sarah Good, who now survived by begging, was once the prosperous daughter of a successful innkeeper. But she was cheated out of her inheritance by her stepfather. She was married to a derelict with whom she had several children, whom she supported by begging for food in an aggressive manner. If refused, Good would turn away cursing and puffing wrathfully on her corncob pipe.

Osburn, the mother of an illegitimate child, had also once been well-to-do as the wife of Robert Prince, owner of a 150-acre farm. When her husband died, she created scandal in Salem by purchasing a young Irish immigrant as an indentured servant. Sarah Osburn paid fifteen pounds—a large sum of money at the time—for the Irishman, Alexander Osburn. The two lived together as husband and wife before getting married. Such an offense was punishable by whipping, and the wedding did not lessen its wickedness. By the time of the accusations, Osburn's money was gone, and she was often sick and bedridden.

Warrants Against the Witches

When their names were announced by the afflicted girls, four men of Salem Village appeared before magistrates (local members of the judiciary) and filled out legal papers (warrants) to arrest the women on suspicion of witchcraft. The men who filed the warrants were Thomas Putnam, his brother Edward Putnam, Joseph Hutchinson, and Thomas Preston. Warrants were issued for the arrest of Tituba, Sarah Good, and Sarah Osburn on February 29, 1692.

The three women were to appear on March 1 at Samuel Ingersoll's tavern. There the magistrates would undertake preliminary examinations concerning the charges against them. The charges were that the three had practiced witchcraft against Elizabeth Parris, Abigail Williams, and two other girls by afflicting them with fits and convulsions. The examinations would determine if there was enough evidence to arrest the suspects and hold formal trials. It was about this time that Samuel Parris removed his daughter Elizabeth from the uproar in Salem Village. He sent her to stay with friends out of town, where she remained until the witchcraft affair was over.

Besides Abigail Williams and Elizabeth Parris, nine other girls and young women were acting strangely. They were called the "afflicted girls." Two of the afflicted were Ann Putnam Sr. and her twelve-year-old daughter, Ann Jr. (The titles "Senior" and "Junior" were sometimes given to women as well as men in the seventeenth century.) Both mother and daughter were high-strung, imaginative, and sensitive women. Ann Sr. was the wife and Ann Jr. the daughter of Thomas Putnam, who was a strong supporter of Reverend Parris in the bitter village fight over granting Parris the parsonage.

The Putnams were a prominent family with great influence in the village. Thus

A woman suspected of being a witch is put under arrest.

young Ann took a leading role in the witchcraft excitement, and the Putnam home became the center of the hysteria. The Putnams' servant, Mercy Lewis, 17, was also afflicted.

The other afflicted girls were Mary Warren, 20, a servant in the John Proctor household; Elizabeth Booth, 18, a village girl who lived near the Proctors; Mary Walcott, 17, daughter of Captain John Walcott, deacon of the parish; Susannah Sheldon, 18, daughter of a village family; Sarah Churchill, 20, a servant in the family of George Jacobs; and Elizabeth Hubbard, 17, a niece of the wife of Dr. Griggs, who diagnosed the original girls as being touched by the Devil. These young women would play a part in the witchcraft hysteria before it was over.

Once the accusations set the wheels of justice in motion, Salem Village witch madness began to spin out of control.

Chapter

3 Making Accusations

On the morning of March 1, 1692, practically everyone in Salem Village and the surrounding area was crowded around Sam Ingersoll's tavern. They were waiting for the magistrates to arrive—and to get a glimpse of the accused witches.

Nothing this exciting had ever happened in the Salem area. Farmers left their fieldwork undone. Children left their chores unattended. Women neglected their cooking and cleaning. People gathered in small groups gossiping about the accused. Many recalled strange incidents that had previously seemed unimportant but now appeared to incriminate the alleged witches.

By the time the magistrates arrived, the crowd had grown too large for the tavern, so the meetinghouse was opened. It too quickly filled with spectators. Before long the preliminary examination got under way.

Publicly Accusing Sarah Good

The three accused women were questioned by two Salem magistrates who went on to conduct the majority of preliminary examinations against the accused witches.

One of the men was John Corwin, the other was John Hathorne, whose great-great-grandson added a *w* to the name and became the well-known author Nathaniel Hawthorne.

Sarah Good was the first to be examined. Hathorne did most of the questioning. He was expected to act like an impartial magistrate gathering facts. But he questioned Good more in the manner of a prosecuting attorney, trying to bully a confession out of the woman. This is obvious in the trial transcripts that were reprinted in Chadwick Hansen's *Witchcraft at Salem*.

> "Sarah Good, what evil spirit have you familiarity with?"
> "None."
> "Have you made no contract with the Devil?"
> "No."
> "Why do you hurt these children?"
> "I do not hurt them. I scorn it."
> "Who do you employ, then, to do it?"
> "I employ nobody."
> "What creature do you employ, then?"
> "No creature, but I am falsely accused."[17]

Hathorne then turned to the afflicted girls and asked them if Sarah Good was the person who had tormented them. The girls said she was, "upon which they were all dreadfully tortured and tormented for a

Nathaniel Hawthorne

Nathaniel Hawthorne was a notable nineteenth-century American novelist who was born in Salem, Massachusetts, on July 4, 1804. His great-great-grandfather John Hathorne conducted the primary examinations of all the people accused of witchcraft in 1692. Hawthorne was the first American author to apply pointed artistic judgment to seventeenth-century Puritan society, which he often did with caustic humor. In his work *The Scarlet Letter*, published in 1850, Hawthorne describes the Puritan women who thronged around a prison courtyard hoping to witness a hanging.

> On the summer morning when our story begins its course . . . the women, of whom there were several in the crowd, appeared to take a peculiar interest in whatever penal infliction might be expected to ensue. . . . The age had not so much refinement, that any sense of impropriety restrained . . . [them] from stepping forth into the public ways, and wedging their not unsubstantial persons . . . into the throng nearest to the scaffold at an execution. Morally, as well as materially, there was a coarser fibre in those wives and maidens of old English birth and breeding . . . for, throughout that chain of ancestry, every successive mother has transmitted to her child a fainter bloom, a more delicate and briefer beauty, and a slighter physical frame, if not a character of less force and solidity, than her own. . . . They were . . . countrywomen; and the beef and ale of their native land, with a moral diet not a whit more refined, entered largely into their composition.

Hawthorne died on May 11, 1864, at the age of fifty-nine, by which time he had published several widely read novels and short stories.

short space of time."[18] When the fits were over the girls said Good had assumed the form of a specter (a ghost) and caused the afflictions.

This accusation of Good using a specter to torment the girls became a central legal issue of the later trials. People in the packed meetinghouse saw the girls' violent physical symptoms with their own eyes. A physician said they were caused by witchcraft. A malicious old woman was accused of causing them. What better answer than the afflictions were caused by Good as revenge for the accusations? Hathorne certainly seemed convinced. He continued:

> "Sarah Good, do you not see now what you have done? Why do you not tell us the truth? Why do you thus torment these poor children?"
> "I do not torment them."
> "Who do you employ, then?"
> "I employ nobody. I scorn it."[19]

When Good was asked who afflicted the children if she did not, the old woman was more than willing to point the finger at her fellow prisoner Sarah Osburn.

Later in the trial, Good's husband, William, stated in court that

> "he was afraid that she either was a witch or would be one very quickly." When [Hathorne] asked if he had any concrete evidence of her practicing witchcraft he replied that he had not; he thought her a witch for "her bad carriage to him." "Indeed," said he, "I may say with tear that she is an enemy to all good."[20]

Two women believed to be witches face their accusers. The trials often included violent displays of physical symptoms and the use of bullying tactics to extract confessions.

William Good went on to offer the court evidence that his wife had a "strange tit or wart" on her body. This was known as the "witch's tit," at which the Devil and his familiars sucked the blood of a witch. After William's testimony ended, Sarah Good's four-year-old daughter, Dorcas, was brought to the stand. The little girl announced that her mother had familiars: "three birds, one black, one yellow, and that these birds hurt the children and afflicted persons."[21]

The clerk who recorded Good's examination noted that "her answers were in a very wicked, spiteful manner, reflecting and retorting against the authority with base and abusive words and many lies."[22]

Examining Sarah Osburn

When Sarah Osburn took the stand, she too denied that she had afflicted the children. But once again, the girls fell into violent fits. Hathorne asked Osburn how this was happening, and the accused said that the Devil might be going about in her likeness doing harm, but she knew nothing of it.

Osburn was then asked why she thought the Devil might be going about in her form, and she recalled that "she was frighted one time in her sleep and either saw or dreamed that she saw a thing like an Indian, all black, which did prick her in her neck and pulled her by the back part of her head to the door of the house." But several of the audience volunteered that Osburn had once said "she would never be tied to that lying spirit any more." This attracted Hathorne's interest, since the Devil is the Prince of Lies. He asked the accused:

"What lying spirit is this? Hath the Devil ever deceived you and been false to you?"
"I do not know the Devil. I never did see him."
"What lying spirit was it then?"
"It was a voice that I thought I heard."
"What did it propound [say] to you?"
"That I should go no more to meeting. But I said I would, and did go the next Sabbath day."[23]

But Hathorne pointed out that Osburn had not been to church recently. The woman said she had been very sick. Osburn's examination ended and afforded grounds for further questioning. The idea suggested by Osburn, that the Devil could work through the specter of an innocent person, would loom large in the months that followed.

Tituba Shocks the Village

The major event on that first of March was Tituba's examination. Just the presence of an Indian in a room full of Puritans created a stir. And Osburn had described her apparition as "a thing like an Indian all black," linking the images of Indians and demons.

Tituba's court appearance was recorded in great detail by reporter Ezekiel Cheever. His transcripts were reprinted in Charles Upham's book *Salem Witchcraft*, written in 1867. Hathorne questioned the frightened woman:

"Tituba, what evil spirit have you familiarity with?"
"None."
"Why do you hurt these children?"

Search for Witch's Marks

Witch-hunters had many dubious means for proving their case against suspected witches. Several common methods were listed in *Witches and Witchcraft,* by the editors of Time-Life Books:

> Witch hunters had means . . . of certifying their prey. For instance, a terrified suspect's inability to weep on demand incriminated her, since witches were thought unable to shed tears. Quite common also was the search for witch's marks—extra nipples at which she supposedly suckled her familiars—and devil's marks, insensitive spots of skin allegedly made by the devil's claws or teeth. Suspects were stripped, shaved from head to toe, then exhaustively examined for blemishes, moles, or scars that could be labeled diabolical. To find marks invisible to the eye, examiners prodded every inch of the accused's body with a bodkin [a small, sharply pointed instrument for making holes in fabric or leather] until they found a spot that did not bleed or feel pain. Scholars now say the emotional shock of being publicly stripped and searched could well have produced areas of temporary anesthesia in some victims, thus providing witch hunters with the "proof" they sought.

A woman is searched for physical marks that could prove she is a witch.

"I do not hurt them."

"Who is it then?"

"The Devil, for aught I know."

"Did you never see the Devil?"

"The Devil," said Tituba, "came to me and bid me serve him."

"Who have you seen?"

"Four women sometimes hurt the children."

"Who were they?"

"Goody Osburn and Sarah Good, and I do not know who the others were. Sarah Good and Osburn would have me hurt the children, but I would not."

[The court clerk wrote:] (She further saith there was a tall man of Boston that she did see.)

"When did you see them?"

"Last night, at Boston."

"What did they say to you?"

"They said, 'Hurt the children.'"

"And did you hurt them?"

"No: there is four women and one man, they hurt the children, and then they lay all upon me; and they tell me, if I will not hurt the children, they will hurt me."

"But did you not hurt them?"

"Yes; but I will hurt them no more."

"What have you seen?"

"A man come to me, and say, 'Serve me.'"

"What service?"

"Hurt the children: and last night there was an appearance that said, 'Kill the children'; and, if I would not go on hurting the children, they would do worse to me."

"What is this appearance you see?"

"Sometimes it is like a hog, and sometimes like a great dog."

[The court clerk writes:] (This appearance she saith she did see four times.)

"What did it say to you?"

"The black dog said, 'Serve me'; but I said, 'I am afraid.' He said, if I did not, he would do worse to me."

"What did you say to it?"

"'I will serve you no longer.' Then he said he would hurt me; and then he looks like a man, and threatens to hurt me."

[The court clerk writes:] (She said that this man had a yellow-bird that kept with him.)

"And he told me he had more pretty things that he would give me, if I would serve him."

"What were these pretty things?"

"He did not show me them."

"What else have you seen?"

"Two cats; a red cat, and a black cat."

"What did they say to you?"

"They said, 'Serve me.'"

"When did you see them?"

"Last night; and they said, 'Serve me'; but I said I would not."

"What service?"

"She said, hurt the children."[24]

Tituba continued that the specter had brought her to Elizabeth Hubbard that morning and that Tituba was made to pinch the girl. Then she was asked about tormenting the other afflicted girls:

"Why did you go to Thomas Putnam's last night, and hurt his child?"

"They pull and haul me, and make go."

"And what would they have you do?"

"Kill her with a knife."

[Ezekiel Cheever writes:] (Lieutenant Fuller and others said at this time, when the child saw these persons, and was tormented by them, that she did complain of a knife,—that they would have her cut her head off with a knife.) "How did you go?"

"We ride upon sticks, and are there presently."

"Do you go through the trees or over them?"

"We see nothing, but are there presently."

"Why did you not tell your master?"

"I was afraid: they said they would cut off my head if I told."

"Would you not have hurt others, if you could?"

"They said they would hurt others, but they could not."

"What attendants hath Sarah Good?"

"A yellow-bird, and she would have given me one."

"What meat did she give it?"

"It did suck her between her fingers. . . ."

"Did you not hurt Mr. Curren's child?"

"What hath Sarah Osburn?"

"Yesterday she had a thing with a head like a woman, with two legs and wings." [Cheever writes:] (Abigail Williams, that lives with her uncle Mr. Parris, said that she did see the same creature, and it turned into the shape of Goodie Osburn.)

"What else have you seen with Osburn?"

"Another thing, hairy: it goes upright like a man, it hath only two legs."[25]

Tituba continued that the Devil had shown her a book with nine red bloodlike marks—two made by Good and Osburn. Good had supposedly confessed to Tituba to making the marks but Osburn would not. Other marks, Tituba claimed, were made by women from Boston whom she did not know.

As Tituba was speaking, the girls once again fell into fits. They claimed that Tituba had been pinching and pricking them during her entire testimony. When the magistrate asked Tituba who was afflicting the girls, the woman said she saw the shape of Sarah Good tormenting them.

During Tituba's final confession, the courtroom became hushed. Even the afflicted girls quieted down. It is not clear why Tituba confessed. Perhaps she saw a way out by telling the court what it wanted to hear. By the end of the examination, Tituba herself began having seizures like those of the girls.

The Aftermath of the Examinations

Tituba's confession was similar to other witchcraft examinations from other times and places. Historians believe that she was told what to say by Reverend Parris and Thomas Putnam. It seems impossible, for example, that Tituba would have known that one of the afflicted girls thought Good would cut her head off with a knife, unless the woman was told this ahead of time. Parris and Putnam wanted to strongly implicate Good and Osburn, and Tituba was the perfect witness for doing so.

Tituba's confession confirmed the worst fears of witchcraft held by the public. It also confirmed the widely held hatred and fear of Good, Osburn, and Tituba. Villagers began to blame the three women for any and all strange events and dreams. One example occurred the night the trial ended. Two villagers, William Allen and John Hughes, were frightened by a strange

The Witch's Broom

Tituba thrilled the Puritans when she told Salem magistrates that she had ridden through the air "upon a stick or pole." This reference fits the now familiar image of a witch flying through the air on a broomstick. The first known illustration of a witch's broom appears in a fifteenth-century Swiss book called *The Champion of Women*. But the magical associations of brooms are far older.

Brooms have long been connected to female magic and power. Along the way they became the equivalent of the magical staff—such as the one Moses reportedly used to part the Red Sea. In ancient Rome, midwives believed sweeping a doorstep would drive evil spirits from the home where a woman was about to deliver a baby. Until the twentieth century, women in England left brooms outside their cottages to safeguard the house when they were out. In gypsy cultures, newlyweds hope for good luck when they jump over a broomstick upon entering a new home. Modern witches leap over a broom as part of a marriage ceremony called handfasting.

As symbols of the pagan past, brooms sometimes aroused the suspicion of witch-hunters. In a report from 1598, a French girl testified that she and her mother had mounted a broom made of twigs. The women then flew up the chimney and were carried through the air.

noise. Then they "saw a strange and unusual beast lying on the ground. . . . Going up to it, the said beast vanished away and in the said place started up two or three women and fled, . . . not after the manner of other women but swiftly vanished out of our sight, which women we took to be Sarah Good, Sarah Osburn and Tituba."[26]

The next night, Allen began to hallucinate: "Sarah Good visibly appeared to him in his chamber, said Allen being in bed, and brought an unusual light in with her. The said Sarah came and sat upon his foot. The said Allen went to kick at her, upon which she vanished and the light with her."[27]

But even more than the fear of the three accused women was the hint in Tituba's testimony that there were other witches yet undiscovered. Hadn't Tituba testified that there were two witches from Boston? And weren't there nine marks in the Devil's book, with only two attributed to Good and Osburn? Tituba's testimony set loose an unprecedented wave of

The Witches' Jail

The jails of Salem and Boston would be described today as torture chambers. Inmates considered the most dangerous—such as witches—were kept in dungeons. These were dark, bitterly cold, and so damp that water ran down the walls. They reeked of unwashed bodies and human waste. All prisoners were forced to suffer inhuman treatment. They were kept hungry and thirsty, and they froze in the winter. Their arms and legs were weighted down, or they were chained to walls so their specter could less easily escape and wreak havoc. Some cells were so tiny that the prisoner could not even sit or lie down.

During the Salem witch hysteria, even the four-year-old Dorcas Good was incarcerated in a Boston prison for alleged witchcraft. The little girl spent months in the darkness, in irons, chained to a wall. According to *A Delusion of Satan* by Frances Hill,

> Eighteen years later, her father, William Good, was to write that "she was in prison seven or eight months and being chained in the dungeon was so hardly used and terrified that she hath ever since been very chargeable, having little or no reason to govern herself."

By "very chargeable" he meant a financial burden: When she came out and for the rest of her days, he had to pay a keeper to care for her.

Witches who were considered enemies of God were treated with extreme cruelty by wardens and demonologists.

An inmate of a witches' jail reads by candlelight. Less fortunate prisoners were chained to walls or weighted down with irons.

paranoia in the tiny community. Villagers began to cast suspicious glances at their neighbors, wondering if they might be witches or wizards.

For the time being, however, there was no witch-hunt. Tituba and Osburn were examined again on March 3, Tituba and Good on March 5. The accusations continued from the afflicted girls. They said that the women had visited them and tortured them by pinching, pricking, biting, and almost choking them to death.

Other charges not specifically related to the girls were also heard in court. Sarah Good, for instance, cursed people for not giving her food and shelter. Various indi-viduals remembered that soon after, their cattle, sheep, or pigs had died or disap-peared. Many of these events had hap-pened years earlier, and had other explanations, but they were brought up in court as proof of witchcraft.

On March 7, the magistrates were satis-fied that Good, Tituba, and Osburn were witches, and thus they were sent to Boston jail. Osburn, already in ill health, was to die there on May 10. Tituba was never brought to trial but was forced to stay in jail because Parris would not pay the jailer's fees to free her. She was later sold to pay the fees. Eventually, Sarah Good was put on trial.

Chapter

4 The Widening Circle

The accusations of witchcraft by Abigail Williams, Betty Parris, and the other afflicted girls led to the imprisonment of Sarah Good, Sarah Osburn, and Tituba. After this outcome, the girls warmed to their game, and it was not long before the circle of accused witches widened to snare more of Salem Village's rich and poor, sinners and saints, women and men.

Suspicion and fear spread through the community like a plague, touching almost every family. Whenever a child fell ill, a cow stopped giving milk, or two neighbors had a dispute, people suspected witchcraft. Those whose behavior was odd or who were despised by the townsfolk suddenly began to look like Satan's handmaidens. Salem quickly plunged into mass hysteria; Abigail and Betty were only too happy to contribute to the mayhem.

Accusing Goodwife Corey

On March 11, 1692, four days after those who were first accused were sent to jail, Salem's leaders declared a day of prayer and fasting. During this time, Salem Village's influential men held a meeting. But the main focus of the day was the behavior of the afflicted girls. They continued to

have hallucinations, with a new specter appearing to haunt them. This time it was not a slave or a despised old woman, but Martha Corey, a member in good standing of the church. Corey was accused by Ann Putnam, daughter of Sergeant Thomas Putnam, who was a parish clerk. Two others who heard the accusations were Edward Putnam—Ann's uncle—and Ezekiel Cheever, whose notes taken in court are the main record of the witch trials that has survived the centuries.

The Putnams and Cheever thought it their duty to go to Martha Corey with the afflicted girl's complaint. The men first asked Ann Putnam what clothes Martha Corey's apparition would be wearing. The reasoning was that Corey would be wearing the clothes seen in the afflicted girl's apparition when the men went to Corey's house. Ann replied that Corey had blinded her and she could not see Corey's clothes. But the apparition told Ann that its name was Corey and that Ann should see it no more before dark. The men took this obvious evasion at face value and went to the house of Giles Corey and his wife, Martha. Cheever describes their encounter in *Witchcraft at Salem:*

And as soon as we came in, in a smiling manner she saith "I know what you are come for; you are come to talk with me

A witness points an accusing finger during her testimony. Some suspects attempted to avoid punishment by claiming that they were put under spells by other members of the colony.

about being a witch, but I am none. I cannot help people's talking of me." Edward Putnam answered her that it was the afflicted person that did complain of her that was the occasion of our coming to her. She presently replied, "But does she tell you what clothes I have on?" We made her no answer to this at her first asking, whereupon she asked again with very great eagerness, "But does she tell you what clothes I have on? . . ." Which question, with that eagerness of mind with which [Corey] did ask, made us to think of what Ann Putnam had told us before we went to her, and we told her no, [Ann] did not, for she told us that you came and blinded her and told her that she should see you no more before it was night, that so she might not tell us what clothes you had on. [Corey] made but little answer to this but seemed to smile at it, as if she had showed us a pretty trick.[28]

Eight days later, on March 19, the Reverend Deodat Lawson arrived in Salem Village. The accusations against Corey were related to him and he spent time with the afflicted girls. The reverend's essay about the witch hysteria, *A Brief and True Narrative . . .* , states that by the time of his arrival there were ten afflicted: three girls from nine to twelve years old: Elizabeth Parris, Abigail Williams, and Ann Putnam; three adolescent girls: Mary Walcott, Mercy Lewis, and Elizabeth Hubbard; and four married women: Goodwives Putnam, Pope, Bibber, and "an ancient woman named" Goodall.

Lawson conducted services on March 20, and several of the afflicted were present. Of them, he wrote:

They had several Sore Fits, in the time of Publick Worship, which did . . . interrupt me in my First Prayer; being so unusual. . . . In Sermon time when [Goodwife Corey] was present in the Meetinghouse

Lawson's Sermon

The unusually named Deodat Lawson had been Salem Village's minister from 1687 until 1691, when Samuel Parris and his witch-accusing daughter and niece arrived. (Lawson's first name was derived from a Latin word meaning "God-given.") When Lawson returned in the midst of the witch hysteria, he preached a sermon called *Christ's Fidelity the Only Shield Against Satan's Malignity,* which he later published. Although the sermon was interrupted repeatedly by the afflicted girls, Lawson still managed to stir the emotions of the community but also warned villagers against acting rashly. The sermon was reprinted with comments in Chadwick Hansen's *Witchcraft at Salem.* In the sermon

> Lawson . . . reaffirm[ed] that the girl's afflictions were the "effects of Diabolical malice and operations, and that it cannot be rationally imagined to proceed from any other cause whatsoever." He . . . urged [the magistrates] to do severe justice "to approve yourselves the terror of and punishment to evildoers, and a praise to them that do well."
>
> Careless accusations of suspected persons might also backfire, Lawson warned. "Rash censuring of others, without sufficient grounds, or false accusing any willingly . . . is indeed to be like the Devil, who . . . is a calumniator [liar], or false accuser." Most important, he warned his listeners that the Devil might appear in the shape of an innocent person. Indeed, he suspected this was precisely what had happened when [the afflicted] saw the apparitions of other church members afflicting them.

In spite of Lawson's urge for caution, the accusations continued for months.

[Abigail Williams] called out, "Look where [Goodwife Corey] sits on the Beam suckling her Yellow bird betwixt her fingers"! Ann Putnam another Girle afflicted said there was a Yellow-bird sat on my hat as it hung on the Pin in the Pulpit: but those that were by, restrained her from speaking loud about it.[29]

The accusations against Corey had now been made public at the services. Two days later, Corey would be arrested and hauled before the magistrates in the Salem meetinghouse.

Corey's Examination

We do not know how Martha Corey knew that the men would try to identify her by her clothes on March 11. She might have heard it from someone who had seen Ann Putnam's fits. In any case, her knowledge of the incident worked against her. At her examination on March 21, Hathorne was even more brutal than he had been with the other suspects. When asked how she knew that the child could not identify the clothes she wore, she said that Cheever had told her. When Cheever denied this, Hathorne erupted: "You dare thus to lie in all this assembly. You are now before authority! I expect the truth. You promised it. Speak now, and tell us who told you [about the] clothes." Corey could only answer, "Nobody."[30]

Corey was also treated harshly because she did not believe the accusations made about Good, Osburn, and Tituba. She had tried to prevent her husband from attending the examination of those women, going so far as to remove the saddle from his horse. And during her own examination she protested that her accusers "were poor, distracted Children, and no heed [should] be given to what they said."[31] When asked if she believed there were any witches in the country, Corey answered that she did not know any. Martha Corey's skepticism was held against her—again, the logic ran that if she denied there were witches, she must be one.

During the examination most of the afflicted were in the meetinghouse. They did

This fragment of the written record of Martha Corey's examination bears the signature of Magistrate John Hathorne.

vehemently accuse [Corey] . . . of afflicting them, by Biting, Pinching, Strangling, etc. And that they did in the Fit see her Likeness coming to them, and bringing a Book to them, she said, she had no Book; they affirmed, she had a Yellow-Bird, that used to suck betwixt her fingers.

When asked about it, Corey replied:

She had no Familiarity with any such thing. She was a Gospel Woman: which Title she called herself by; and the Afflicted Persons told her, ah! She was a Gospel Witch. Ann Putnam did there affirm . . . she saw the shape of [Goodwife Corey] Praying . . . to the Devil.[32]

As in the other examinations, the afflicted claimed that the alleged witch was torturing them during the trial. According to Lawson:

It was observed several times, that if [Corey] did but bite her [lower] lip in time of Examination the persons afflicted were bitten on their armes and wrists and produced the Marks before the Magistrates, Ministers and others. And being watched for that, if she did but Pinch her Fingers, or Graspe one hand hard in another, they were Pinched and produced the Marks before the Magistrates, and Spectators.[33]

How Corey managed to produce bite marks on the afflicted is a matter of debate. Hysterical people are very suggestible, so it is possible that whenever Corey bit her lip, the hysterical girls felt they were being bitten. The girls also might have inflicted the marks on themselves while they were not observed. In addition, skin lesions are among the commonest of psychosomatic symptoms (physical symptoms originating from mental or emotional causes). In any event, the tortures continued, and one of the afflicted women, a Mrs. Pope, reacted violently:

Particularly Mrs. Pope complained of grievous torment in her bowels as if they were torn out. She vehemently accused [Corey] as the instrument, and first threw her Muff at her; but that flying not home, she got off her Shoe, and hit Goodwife [Corey] on the head with it. After these postures were watched, if [Corey] did but stir her feet, they were afflicted in their Feet, and stamped fearfully.

Finally the afflicted people asked Corey why she did not go to the witches who were mustering in front of the meetinghouse. Lawson continues:

Did [Corey] not hear the Drumbeat? They accused her of having Familiarity with the Devil, in the time of Examination, in the shape of a Black man whispering in her ear. . . . They told her, she had Covenanted with the Devil for ten years, six of them were gone, and four more to come. She was required by the Magistrates to answer that Question in the Catechism, "How many persons be there in the God-Head?" She answered it but oddly, yet was there no great thing to be gathered from it; she denied all that was charged upon her.[34]

Corey's protests were futile. After the examination ended, she was taken to the Salem prison. After she was committed, the afflicted claimed that Corey no longer appeared in apparitions or tortured them.

White Magic in Salem

For centuries, witches were believed to practice black—or bad—magic and white—or good—magic. But witches were not the only ones who used spells and charms in everyday life, such as the egg and glass experiment practiced by Abigail Williams, Elizabeth Parris, and Tituba. Another common divining method was enacted with a pair of scissors and a sieve or tea strainer. Like a modern Ouija board, two persons held the handle of the open scissors while the sieve was suspended between the points. Questions were asked and the answer depended on the movement of the sieve over the words in a Bible, newspaper, or other book. Another common method of divining was the key and Bible, in which a key was inserted between the pages of a Bible and the answers to questions were found in the words to which the key pointed.

One of the commonest ways to counteract spells allegedly cast upon an animal was to cut off a piece of the ailing animal—usually an ear—and burn it or boil it. This might also be done for a sick child—not cutting his or her ear, of course, but by burning or boiling a lock of the child's hair.

This practice verged on black magic because it not only broke a witch's spell but could also be used to injure someone. To cast a spell on another, a witch might cut a lock of the target's hair and burn it.

Accusing Rebecca Nurse and a Four-Year-Old Girl

The people of Salem Village soon realized that the suspicion of witchcraft would not end with Goodwife Corey. Word spread through town that Deodat Lawson had been present when Rebecca Nurse's specter also appeared to Abigail Williams on Saturday, March 19. This accusation shocked villagers perhaps more than any other. Rebecca Nurse was an unlikely witch. She was an elderly, gentle woman known for her piety and goodness. She lived on a huge farm surrounded by her many children and grandchildren. Although she and her husband came from modest means, by hard work and good business sense, they had become successful landowners.

The obvious prosperity of the Nurse family caused resentment among Salem villagers. Moreover, the Nurses kept to themselves and had taken a doubting attitude toward the bewitched girls. Many townsfolk felt this showed a lack of concern for the alleged victims.

When Rebecca Nurse was brought to the meetinghouse on March 24, the girls were there to greet her. They were twisting and turning—screaming out that Goodwife Nurse was tormenting them. But this time the magistrates had a difficult time believing that their suspect could be a witch. It was the first time Magistrate Hathorne was unsure of himself. His tone was completely different than it had been with Corey and the others. He told Nurse, "I pray God clear you if you be innocent, and if you be guilty discover you."[35]

Like the others, Nurse pled innocent, but her every movement caused incredible torment in the afflicted. According to Lawson:

[Nurse's] motions did produce like effects as to Biteing, Pinching, Bruising, Tormenting, at their Breasts by her Leaning, and when, bended Back, were as if their Backs were broken. The afflicted persons said, the Black man whispered to [Nurse] . . . and therefore she could not hear what the Magistrates said unto her. . . . [The girls] grievously afflicted, so that there were such an hideous scriech [screech] and noise . . . as did amaze me.[36]

The afflicted claimed there were birds flying around Nurse. Whichever way she moved, the girls, acting together, took the same position. Mary Walcott testified that in the past, Nurse had been responsible for the death of several villagers. Finally, like the others, Nurse was carted off to Boston jail.

One more person was arrested that day, and this showed how quickly the madness was spreading. The newest accused witch was Dorcas Good, the four-year-old daughter of Sarah Good. The little girl was

The Nurse house, which was located on a huge farm outside of Salem Village.

brought before the afflicted, and, once again, the accusers claimed that they were being bitten by the child and showed tiny teeth marks to prove it. Like the others, the young child was taken to prison in chains.

On March 26, Dorcas Good was examined by the magistrates. During the examination she told the men she "had a Snake that used to Suck on the lowest Joynt of [her] Fore-Finger . . . where they Observed a deep Red Spot, about the Bigness of a Flea-bite, they asked who gave [her] that Snake . . . her Mother did."[37]

The red spot observed by the men was probably a flea bite. But the confession of Dorcas was taken at face value. In addition she said her mother had given her the familiar in the form of the snake. This must have horrified the magistrates. If a four-year-old girl was suckling demons, the Devil must have a strong foothold in Massachusetts.

The Next Victims

While witch hysteria was spreading throughout the village, only one man, John Proctor, spoke out against it. The morning after Nurse and Dorcas Good were taken away, Proctor appeared in the village in a rage. He had come to take home his servant, Mary Walcott, one of the afflicted girls. He expressed his opinion of the afflicted girls' testimony: "If they were let alone [to continue] we should all be devils and witches quickly. They should rather be [tied] to the whipping post. But he would take his [servant girl] home and thrash the Devil out of her."[38] Almost immediately, the afflicted

Magistrate Hathorne's signature appears again on this portion of Rebecca Nurse's record of examination.

girls began to see the specter of John Proctor's wife, Elizabeth.

John Proctor was not the only person to show scorn for the afflicted girls. Nurse's sister Sarah Cloyse had an unprecedented outburst in church. On Sunday, April 3, Reverend Parris used a biblical quotation in his sermon taken from John 6:70—"Have I not chosen you twelve, and one of you is a Devil."[39] This was directed at Nurse, and the implication was that the old woman was the Devil. This was too much for Sarah Cloyse. She walked out of the meetinghouse and slammed the door behind her. The congregation was amazed. Such a public expression of resentment in the midst of a church service was unheard of.

Within hours, the afflicted girls began seeing the apparition of Sarah Cloyse taking the Devil's sacrament of "Red bread and drink."[40] This was the third time in four days that the girls had mentioned the witches' sacrament. Now the community was no longer thinking in terms of single witches, but of an organized society of witches with its own structure and sacraments.

On April 4, Sarah Cloyse and Elizabeth Proctor were charged with witchcraft. On April 8, warrants were issued for their arrest. On April 11, five men from Boston joined the local magistrates in examining the new suspects. Because it took a week for the examinations to begin, and because more magistrates were brought in to oversee the trials, it appeared that these examinations would be taken more seriously by the villagers. One of the new magistrates was a very important man—Thomas Danforth, deputy governor of the colony.

Cloyse's actions during the trial were opposite from those of her meek sister. When John Indian accused her of hurting him, Cloyse said, "Oh, you are a grievous liar." But when she was accused of drinking blood at a witches' meeting with Sarah Good and the others, Cloyse slumped into her seat. She received no sympathy, the girls jeered, "Her spirit has gone to prison to her sister Nurse."[41]

The presence of the new magistrates did nothing to calm the chaos in the room. The hysterical girls screamed accusations, fell into seizures, and rolled on the floor. When John Proctor tried to defend his wife, the girls began to accuse him. In the end, he was committed to jail, along with his wife. With the jailing of the Proctors, complete ruin came to their family. In 1700, Robert Calef wrote of what happened to the Proctors in the book *More Wonders of the Invisible World*:

> John Procter and his Wife being in Prison, the Sheriff came to his House and seized all the Goods, Provisions, and Cattle that he could come at, and sold some of the Cattle at half price, and killed others . . . ; threw out the Beer out of a Barrel, and carried away the Barrel; emptied a Pot of Broath [soup], and took away the Pot, and left nothing in the house for the support of the Children: No part of the said Goods are known to be returned.[42]

Accusing an Afflicted Girl

The introduction of magistrates from the highest colonial court in Boston had increased the importance of the witchcraft affair and widened its scope to include the entire colony. On April 18, warrants were issued for three more witches and a wizard. They were Abigail Hobbs, Bridget Bishop, and to everyone's surprise, one of the afflicted girls, Mary Warren, the Proctors' servant. Also included was Giles Corey, husband of Martha Corey.

Mary Warren had stopped with her afflictions when John Proctor threatened to beat her. Warren told all who would listen: "When I was afflicted I thought I saw apparitions of a hundred persons."[43] Her head had been "distempered," she said. Now that she was well again, she could not say that she saw any of the apparitions.

John Proctor and his wife lost their house (pictured) and the rest of their belongings after being found guilty of witchcraft.

Soon Warren's words reached the afflicted girls, who accused her of signing the Devil's book.

When she was examined on April 19, Warren's accusers fell into convulsions. When John Indian and Mrs. Pope joined the afflicted, Warren could take it no longer. She too fell into convulsions. Finally her agony was so great she was taken from the courtroom.

Warren was kept in jail for three weeks. The magistrates questioned her from time to time, but she continued to fall into seizures. The magistrates told her they were only interested in her confession that she entered a covenant with the Devil. Finally, hounded by the men and wracked with seizures, she confessed to witchcraft and thoroughly implicated the Proctors. After this, she was quietly released from jail, after which she rejoined the ranks of the afflicted and expressed no more doubts about witchcraft.

Meanwhile, Giles Corey, Abigail Hobbs, and Bridget Bishop were also examined on April 19. Corey and Bishop maintained their innocence, but the girls had fits whenever the accused looked at them. At an earlier time, Hobbs had boasted that she "had sold her body and soul to the old boy [the Devil]."[44] Now she confessed to a large variety of witchcraft and admitted attending witches masses in Mr. Parris's pasture while eating red bread and drinking red wine.

Hobbs named nine persons who were also suspected witches. Among them were her parents, William and Deliverance Hobbs; Mary Easty; another sister of Rebecca Nurse; and Susannah Martin. When it was over, Corey, Hobbs, and Bishop were sent to jail.

When it came time for the examination of Deliverance Hobbs, the woman broke down. When the girls fell into their usual convulsions, Hobbs began to doubt herself. The evidence seemed convincing, and she was not sure she had not done the things she was accused of. She admitted acts of witchcraft and named other guilty persons as well. Her husband, William, on the other hand, proudly maintained his innocence. It did not matter; he too was sent to prison.

The Clergyman Turned Wizard

Reverend George Burroughs was the minister of Salem Village from 1680 to 1682. At the time of the witch hysteria, Burroughs was serving as a minister in Wells, Maine. His time in Salem had not been happy. He had trouble collecting his salary, and many people had been unfriendly to him. In addition, his second wife had died during his time there.

Burroughs's nine-year absence from Salem did not protect him from the accusation by Ann Putnam Jr., who was only two years old when Burroughs left. Like other apparitions, Burroughs's spirit tortured Putnam. But this apparition also told Putnam that he had killed his first two wives. Two weeks later, Burroughs's late wives appeared before Putnam and told her the reverend had "been a cruel man . . . and their blood did cry for vengeance." Burroughs's specter appeared before a number of other people and also told them he had killed his first two wives. Burroughs *had* been cruel to his wives, and Putnam must have heard the villagers gossiping about it.

Marshals from Massachusetts rode to Maine and arrested Burroughs on charges of wizardry. He was examined on May 9, 1692. At his trial, according to *The Salem Witchcraft Delusion,* by Alice Dickinson, the girl accused

> Burroughs of being the leader of the witches' meetings. He blew a trumpet to summon the witches to Mr. Parris's pasture. . . . The trumpet could be heard for miles, but only by witches. Deliverance Hobbs verified the . . . story and said she had been at meetings where Burroughs had urged the witches to bewitch the whole town but do it gradually.

After the examination, Burroughs was taken to Boston jail.

Mary Easty, unlike Hobbs, faced the magistrates with courtesy and a calm demeanor. Although the magistrates were impressed with the accused woman, Easty was sent to prison anyway. In jail, however, she continued to conduct herself with such good manners that the jailer released her. After she had been home for three days, however, Mercy Lewis was seized with such a violent fit that neighbors feared for her life. She moaned the name of Mary Easty. The other girls confirmed that Easty was torturing Lewis, so Easty was returned at once to prison.

Susannah Martin, on the other hand, showed impatience and laughed at the afflicted girls, accusing them of lying. "A false tongue will never make a guilty person,"[45] she said. She too was hauled off to jail.

Witches Far and Wide

With Martin, Easty, and the others behind bars, the accusations continued. Thomas Putnam and his friends were responsible for making twenty complaints against alleged witches in May and June 1692. One complaint listed eight suspects, another eleven. Records have been lost or destroyed, so it is impossible to determine how many were accused by Putnam alone. Most of these suspects were people who had reputations for witchcraft, were relatives of those already in jail, or enemies of the Putnams. The madness had also spread beyond Salem Village to dozens of neighboring towns.

The suspects ranged from the seventy-five-year-old George Jacobs, who could walk only with the aid of crutches, to Elizabeth Carey, the wife of an extremely wealthy merchant. The course of the accusations was the same in each case: The afflicted cried out in torture, the suspect's apparitions were seen signing a covenant with the Devil, and they had partaken in eating the Devil's cake.

As the number of prisoners increased, despair spread throughout eastern Massachusetts. Spring was turning to summer. Crops went unplanted, and farm animals went untended. Hundreds of people had relatives in jail. They had to sell their worldly possessions to pay their relative's jail fees, and they had to travel long distances to visit them. Those who could not pay the fees had their property confiscated. Often their children were evicted from their homes, leaving them to beg for food. Witch hysteria was at its peak, and the actual trials of the witches had not yet begun.

Chapter

5 The Witch Trials

By the end of May 1692, Massachusetts jails were overflowing with more than one hundred people accused of witchcraft. The colony was in an uproar over this witch madness, but little could be done. Because of political changes in England, which governed Massachusetts, the colony had not had a legal charter since 1689. As a result, the legal system devised by the Puritans did not have any true authority, so trials could not be held. This situation left the accused witches in prison awaiting their trials. The situation changed in mid-May 1692, when Increase Mather returned from England bearing the colony's new charter.

When Mather returned, he brought with him Sir William Phipps, his hand-picked nominee for governor. In addition to Phipps, all the other members of the new Massachusetts government were allies of Mather. Writing in his diary, Increase's son Cotton could not hide his joy:

> All the councillors of the province are of my father's nomination and my father-in-law, with several related unto me, and several bretheren of my own church are among them. The governor of the province is not *my enemy* but one whom I baptized, namely Sir William Phipps, one of my own flock, and one of my dearest friends.[46]

The English king granted Phipps the governorship because of Phipps's extensive military experience. As far as England was concerned, the main problem facing the colonies was not witchcraft but rather the threat of war with the French, aided by the Indians. But Phipps was willing to follow Mather's Puritan hard-line policies in matters of religion.

Assembling a Court

When Phipps stepped off the ship in Massachusetts, he found the jails in Boston, Salem, and nearby Ipswich overflowing with witches. Moreover, the complaints, arrests, and examinations were adding more suspects every day. Phipps later wrote of the afflicted girls and witch hysteria as he understood it:

> When I first arrived I found this Province miserably harassed with the most Horrible witchcraft or Possession of Devils which had broke in upon several Townes, some scores of poor people were taken with preternatural torments some scalded with brimstone some had pins stuck in their flesh others hurried into the fire and water and

When he returned from England in 1692, Increase Mather (pictured) brought with him a new legal charter for the Massachusetts Bay Colony and a new governor to enforce it.

some dragged out of their houses and carried over the tops of trees and hills for many Miles together.[47]

With the efficiency of a military man, Phipps wasted no time. On May 27, the governor appointed an emergency court of judges to hold trials for the accused. It was an ad hoc court (one formed for the one specific purpose) called a Court of Oyer and Terminer (meaning "to hear and determine"). In England, this type of emergency court was set up for cases of social disorder on the scale of revolutions and riots. The legality of using a Court of Oyer and Terminer for witch trials was doubtful. But Phipps claimed the court was founded because "of the loud cries and clamours of the friends of the afflicted people."[48] These loud cries Phipps wrote about were undoubtedly Thomas Putnam and his allies—the chief accusers—who were pressing hard to bring the alleged witches to trial.

Phipps appointed members of his governing council to the Court of Oyer and Terminer. All were experienced magistrates who were instructed to reach final verdicts in their cases. No appeals would be granted. The new deputy governor, William Stoughton, was made chief justice of the court. Other judges were Wait Winthrop, Peter Sargent, John Richards, and Samuel Sewall, all from Boston, Bartholemew Gedney of Salem, and Nathaniel Saltonstall of Haverhill. According to Chadwick Hansen in *Witchcraft at Salem:* "No more experienced or distinguished a court could have been assembled anywhere in English America."[49]

Once the court was seated, Phipps was satisfied that the witchcraft matter would be settled. The new governor left Boston to take charge of military operations against the French and Native Americans on the colony's frontier.

Bishop Is Sentenced to Hang

On May 31, the new attorney general, Thomas Newton, ordered nine witches to be transported from Salem to Boston for trial. They were Sarah Good, Rebecca Nurse, John Willard, John and Elizabeth Proctor, Susannah Martin, Bridget Bishop, Alice Parker, and Tituba. Newton specified that Tituba be separated from the rest, since she was coming to give evidence

The Law Against Witchcraft

By modern standards it seems ridiculous to put people on trial for malicious acts to which there were no eyewitnesses. But the law was perfectly clear. Witchcraft had been a criminal offense in England since 1542. According to *More Wonders of the Invisible World,* written by Robert Calef in 1700, the law specifies as follows:

> One that shall use, practise, or exercise any invocation or conjuration of any evil or wicked spirit, or consult, covenant with, entertain or employ, feed or reward any evil or wicked spirit, to or for any intent or purpose; or take up any dead man, woman, or child, out of his, her, or their grave, or any other place, where the dead body resteth; or the skin, bone, or other part of any dead person, to be employed or used in any manner of witchcraft, sorcery, charm or enchantment; or shall use, practise, or exercise any witchcraft, enchantment, charm, or sorcery, whereby any person shall be killed, destroyed, wasted, consumed, pined, or lamed in his or her body, or any part thereof: such offenders duly and lawfully convicted and attainted, shall suffer death.

against the others, not to be tried herself. The order was given in a long, agitated letter that treated the matter as a national emergency. The populace was thrilled at this exciting situation.

The building excitement reached a climax when the General Court declared May 26 as a fast day as a measure against witchcraft throughout Massachusetts. Prayer and fasting had always been the Puritans' first reaction against attacks by the Devil, but such days were usually local affairs. A court-ordered fast for the entire colony was extremely unusual and proved the seriousness of the situation.

The court opened on June 2 and tried one person—Bridget Bishop. As in all the following trials, the suspect had no lawyer. By custom, the judges were supposed to protect the rights of the accused, but they did not. The defendants were treated the same as they had been in the preliminary examinations. The afflicted writhed, moaned, and shrieked. Testimony was given concerning matters that ranged far from the actual charges. The audience shouted comments.

The court was disorderly, and the defendants were presumed guilty before their trials even began.

Bishop had long been rumored to be a witch, and had been earlier accused of bewitching horses and turning herself into a cat. Even her husband accused her. In fact, the accused woman might have practiced black magic. Some years earlier, when tearing down a wall of her house, workmen had "found several puppets made up of rags and hogs' bristles with headless pins in them with the points outward."[50] A doll with pins stuck in it is a classic black magic charm meant to cause harm to an enemy that is represented by the doll.

A freakish incident provided a final piece of damning evidence that was entered against Bishop. When she was taken past the Salem Village meetinghouse on the way to her trial, a board had fallen from the ceiling. This was taken as hard evidence that her demons had invisibly entered the building and pulled part of it down.

It was no accident that Bishop was the first to go to trial. The dolls and the odd events were considered hard evidence. This was proof of witchcraft that went beyond the cries and moans of the afflicted, which Increase Mather had warned against relying on for convictions.

Before the trial had even begun, Cotton Mather gave the judges his advice on proper trial procedure. In a letter, Mather wrote:

I must . . . beg you that . . . you do not lay more stress upon pure specter testimony than it will bear. . . . It is very certain that the devils have sometimes represented the shapes of persons not only innocent but very virtuous. . . .

Moreover, I do suspect that persons who have too much indulged themselves in malignant, envious, malicious, ebullitions [violent outpouring of emotion] of their souls may unhappily expose themselves to judgment of being represented by devils, of whom they never had any vision, and with whom they have much less written a covenant.

Now first a credible confession of the guilty witches is one of the most hopeful ways of coming at them, and I say credible confession because even confession itself sometimes is not credible.[51]

Mather ended the letter suggesting that some of the accused be given a penalty less than death. In any case, the twelve-man jury found Bishop guilty and sentenced her to hang from the neck until dead upon Gallows Hill in Salem on June 10.

Not everyone was satisfied that Bridget Bishop was a witch, however. Nathaniel Saltonstall resigned from the panel. This exposed him to later charges that he too was a witch, though he was never arrested. Jonathan Corwin was appointed to take Saltonstall's place on the court.

Debate over Specters as Evidence

Most seventeenth-century courts in Europe executed anyone who confessed to the crime of witchcraft. But the Puritans in Massachusetts believed in spiritual rebirth and thought that confession was the first step toward moral revival. Therefore, confessors such as Tituba and Dorcas Good were never brought to trial. The court was also trying to follow Mather's advice by not relying on spectral evidence for conviction. But only Bridget Bishop *had* any concrete evidence against her (the dolls with pins).

After the hanging of Bishop, the court took a recess in order to decide what to do next. Several questions were troubling the judges. Almost all of the witches had been jailed after the afflicted girls claimed the suspects' specters had tortured them. The main evidence against them was the bizarre behavior of the girls in the courtroom. But the specters were invisible to all but the bewitched girls. There was little doubt that the girls were in pain. But was spectral evidence enough to sentence a person to death? And might not the Devil take the shape of an innocent person as some of the suspects had suggested? Other evidence against the accused hardly seemed like capital offenses: They had yelled at their neighbors and been held responsible afterward when something bad happened to them.

The judges asked for advice from the Boston clergy. On June 15, 1692, the clergy's reply arrived. In a polite letter, the clergymen sympathized with the afflicted persons and commended the magistrates for their efforts. They recommended that the court treat the afflicted tenderly, with "as little as is possible of such noise, company and openness as may too hastily expose them." But they changed tone when speaking of the suspected witches. The reverends urged "speedy and vigorous prosecution of [those who] have rendered themselves obnoxious [practicing witchcraft]."[52]

The chief justice, William Stoughton, however, was insistent that spectral evidence be allowed. He firmly believed that the Devil would appear only in the form of a guilty person, never an innocent one. When the trials resumed, spectral evidence was allowed.

The Twisted Trial of Rebecca Nurse

On June 30, the court sessions resumed. Five people were tried: Sarah Good, Susannah Martin, Sarah Wild, Elizabeth Howe, and Rebecca Nurse. At these trials, the cries of the afflicted girls were given more weight than they were in the Bishop trial. Not only did the girls go into fits when the accused were brought into the courtroom, but their tortures during the earlier preliminary examinations were brought forth as hard evidence. Fifteen others, besides the afflicted, testified against Howe. Almost as many testified against Martin. Fewer testified against the rest of the suspects. But the performance of the afflicted was the most important evidence, and the girls' behaviors were the same throughout.

The trial with the most twists and turns was that of Rebecca Nurse. The weak old woman, head of a large and prosperous family, was overwhelmed by the proceedings, but she had her allies. In May, thirty-nine people had signed a petition on behalf of the respected Rebecca Nurse. It said, "We never had any cause or grounds to suspect her of any such thing as she is now accused of."[53] Among the signers were several important and influential men who knew they were putting themselves in great danger by siding with an accused witch. One of the signers was John Putnam, who had sworn out the orig-

Lies as Testimony

All appeals to the judges for fairness and accuracy in the witch trials fell on deaf ears. During the trial of five alleged witches, the evidence, cries, and accusations of the afflicted girls reached absurd proportions. Anything the girls said—including obvious lies—was used as hard evidence against the accused.

During Sarah Good's trial, for example, one of the girls cried out that the suspect had stabbed her in the chest with a knife. The young girl even produced a broken blade and said that it was from Good. A young man promptly came forward, however, and said that he had broken his knife the day before and thrown the blade away. He said the afflicted girl was standing nearby. He took out the handle of his broken knife which fit perfectly with the blade the afflicted girl had in her hand. But instead of being thrown out of court, the girl was simply told not to lie, and she continued to give evidence.

At another trial, one of the girls screamed that Boston's leading minister, Reverend Samuel Willard, was afflicting her. She *was* thrown out of the court, but only temporarily. The judges simply announced it was a case of mistaken identity.

At Rebecca Nurse's trial, Nurse's daughter Sarah saw an afflicted woman pull pins out of her clothes and stick them into her knees. The afflicted woman then cried out that Nurse had pinched her. This too was ignored by the judges, who soon condemned Nurse to death.

inal complaint against Nurse, but had since changed his mind.

The jury too must have found it hard to believe that Nurse was a witch. They found her obvious goodness and respectable manner more believable than the girls' writhing and screaming. The jury found Nurse innocent of all charges. But when the verdict was announced, according to Robert Calef's book *More Wonders of the Invisible World:*

Immediately all the accusers in the court . . . made a hideous out-cry, to the amazement not only of the Spectators but the Court also seemed strangely surprised.[54]

Considering how loud the afflicted girls' previous noise had been, this outcry must have been amazing indeed. It struck terror in the hearts of the judges, who believed the jury had made a mistake. The noise went beyond the courtroom and spread to the large crowd that was milling around outside the building. By this time, the hysteria had spread to such a degree that hundreds whose names will never be known were claiming to be afflicted. Those gathered outside, upon hearing news of the innocent verdict, went as wild as the girls inside.

One of the judges stated that the verdict was not satisfactory. Another walked off the bench and threatened to have Nurse retried. Stoughton asked the jury if they had considered the remark Nurse

Chief Justice William Stoughton insisted that spectral evidence be allowed as evidence in the witch trials.

had made when Deliverance Hobbs testified against her. According to Calef:

> When one Hobbs, who had confessed her self to be a Witch, was brought into the Court to witness against her, the Prisoner (Nurse) turning her head to her said, "What, do you bring her? she is one of us," or [words] to that effect.[55]

Nurse's words were interpreted by Stoughton to mean that Hobbs was a witch ("she is one of us"). The jury went out again but could not agree. They decided to question Nurse to ask her what she meant. Nurse did not reply. The men then assumed that Nurse was confirming Stoughton's suggestion. The jury changed the verdict to guilty and sentenced Nurse to hang.

Nurse later wrote a declaration to the court to straighten out the matter, saying:

> I intended no otherways, then [that] they were Prisoners with us, and therefore . . . do judge them not legal Evidence against their fellow Prisoners. And I being something hard of hearing, and full of grief, none informing me how the Court took up my words, and therefore had no opportunity to declare what I intended, when I said they were of our Company.[56]

It was perfectly natural for Nurse to speak of Hobbs as "one of our company," since they had been crowded together in jail. And it was clear that the woman was so overwhelmed by anxiety that she had not heard the jury's questions. But Nurse's declaration was ignored.

The zealous minister Nicholas Noyes had Nurse excommunicated (expelled) from Salem church that very afternoon.

She was brought in chains to the Salem meetinghouse to suffer further humiliation while the excommunication proceeded. This also meant certain damnation in hell for Nurse according to her Puritan beliefs.

Another bitter twist took place before Nurse's execution. Governor Phipps granted the old woman a reprieve. However, the afflicted girls "renewed their outcries against her; insomuch that the governor was by some Salem gentlemen prevailed with to recall the reprieve, and she was executed with the rest."[57] On July 19, the obviously innocent Rebecca Nurse was hanged with the other five witches convicted that week.

A Plea for Sanity

The hanging of Rebecca Nurse must have deflated what little hope the other suspects might have had. She had the best reputation and was the most devoutly Puritan of any of the accused. If authorities would hang her, after a governor's reprieve, what hope was there for anyone else? Four days after the execution, John Proctor, who was to be tried next, addressed a letter on behalf of himself and his fellow prisoners to Increase Mather and four other members of the Boston clergy. According to Calef in *More Wonders,* the letter read in part:

> The innocency of our Case with the Enmity [hatred] of our Accusers and our Judges, and Jury, whom nothing but our Innocent Blood will serve their turn, having Condemned us already before our Tryals, being so much incensed and engaged against us by the Devil, makes us bold to Beg and Implore your Favourable Assistance of this our Humble Petition to his Excellency, That if it be possible our Innocent Blood may be spared, which undoubtedly otherwise will be shed, if the Lord doth not mercifully step in. The Magistrates, Ministers, [Juries] and all the People in general, being so much inraged and incensed against us by the Delusion of the Devil, which we can term no other, by reason we know in our own Consciences, we are all Innocent Persons.

The letter then stated that five confessed witches had accused Proctor and the others "of being along with them at a Sacrament" even though Proctor and the others were in "close Prison." Two of the young suspects had only confessed because "they tyed them Neck and Heels till the Blood was ready to come out of their Noses." The torture continued for Proctor's son who

> because he would not confess that he was Guilty, when he was Innocent, they tyed him Neck and Heels till the Blood gushed out at his Nose, and would have kept him so 24 Hours, if one more Merciful than the rest, had not taken pity on him, and caused him to be unbound.[58]

Proctor's pleading letter did not help him or the others in any way. Neither did a petition, signed by thirty-one people on behalf of Proctor's wife, which said that "God may permit Satan to personate dissemble and thereby abuse innocents. . . . As to what we have ever seen or heard of [John and Elizabeth Proctor]—upon our consciences we judge them innocent of the crime objected."[59]

The Constable, the Minister, and Others

The Proctors were brought to trial on August 5, 1692, along with Reverend George Burroughs, Martha Carrier, George Jacobs Sr., and John Willard.

Willard was a Salem Village constable who had refused to arrest certain people for witchcraft. He fled to Nashawag, now Lancaster, forty miles away, but was arrested there. One of the pieces of evidence at Willard's trial came from an eighty-one-year-old man who claimed Willard was responsible for a bout with painful bladder trouble.

The Proctors, old George Jacobs, and the outspoken Martha Carrier were all skeptics of the witch-hunt. But their importance paled next to George Burroughs. The minister was seen as being the leader in the Devil's campaign to capture Salem Village—and all of New England. The trial was so important, in fact, that Increase Mather attended. Eight confessed witches stated that Burroughs was "head actor at some of their hellish rendezvouses" and "nine persons" bore witness to his "extraordinary lifting and such feats of strength as could not be done without diabolical assistance."[60] The afflicted retold their stories from the preliminary examination, and like the others, Burroughs was sentenced to hang.

Abundant spectral evidence was brought in against Martha Carrier. In 1693, Cotton Mather wrote of the afflicted in *The Wonders of the Invisible World*:

> Martha Carrier, or her Shape . . . Grievously Tormented them, by Biting, Pricking, Pinching, and Choaking of them. . . . While this Carrier was on her Examination . . . the Poor People were so Tortured that every one expected their Death upon the very Spott.[61]

Carrier was accused by witnesses of "strangely bewitching" cattle, killing cows, causing swollen feet in a neighbor, and causing other aches and pains in villagers. Mather ends his essay on Carrier with the words: "The Rampant Hag, Martha Carrier . . . should be Queen of Hell."[62]

As Proctor had guessed, none of the accused had a chance for acquittal. All were found guilty. Elizabeth Proctor's life was spared because she was pregnant. The rest were sentenced to hang on August 19.

The title page of Cotton Mather's The Wonders of the Invisible World.

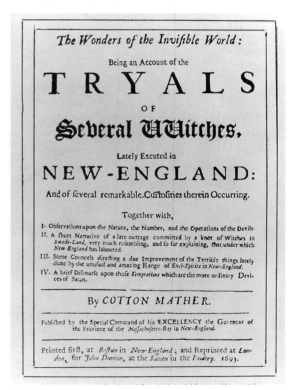

The Wonders of the Invisible World:

Being an Account of the

TRYALS

OF

Several Witches,

Lately Excuted in

NEW-ENGLAND:

And of several remarkable Curiosities therein Occurring.

Together with,

I. Observations upon the Nature, the Number, and the Operations of the Devils.

II. A short Narrative of a late outrage committed by a knot of Witches in *Swede-Land*, very much resembling, and so far explaining, that under which *New-England* has laboured.

III. Some Councels directing a due Improvement of the Terrible things lately done by the unusual and amazing Range of *Evil-Spirits* in *New-England*.

IV. A brief Discourse upon those *Temptations* which are the more ordinary Devices of Satan.

By COTTON MATHER.

Published by the Special Command of his EXCELLENCY the Governour of the Province of the *Massachusetts-Bay* in *New-England*.

Printed first, at *Boston* in *New-England*; and Reprinted at *London*, for *John Dunton*, at the *Raven* in the *Poultrey*. 1693.

Emotions flare during George Jacobs's trial. Jacobs was eventually hanged and his family lost everything they owned.

Immediately after the trial, the sheriff and his officers went to old George Jacob's home and seized everything the family owned, including his wife's wedding ring. The old woman was forced to buy back provisions from the sheriff to feed and clothe herself. The food quickly ran out and Goodwife Jacobs was forced to beg food from the neighbors for the rest of her days.

The Madness Continues

Robert Calef, who wrote extensively of the witch trials in 1700, dryly notes how the proceedings continued:

> September 9. Six more were tried, and received Sentance of Death, viz. Martha Cory of Salem-Village, Mary Easty of Topsfield, Alice Parker and Ann Pudeater of Salem, Dorcas Hoar of Beverly, and Mary Bradberry of Sal-isbury. September 16, Giles Cory was prest to Death.

> September 17. Nine more received Sentance of Death, viz. Margaret Scot of Rowly, Goodwife [Wilmot] Redd of Marblehead, Samuel Wardwell, and Mary Parker of Andover, also Abigail Falkner of Andover, who pleaded Pregnancy, Rebecka Eames of Boxford, Mary Lacy, and Ann Forester of Andover, and Abigail Hobbs of Topsfield. Of these Eight were Executed.[63]

Dorcas Hoar escaped the hangman's noose by accusing others. Mary Bradbury was a wealthy woman in Salisbury who had a long-running feud with Ann Putnam's father, who had spread rumors that Bradbury was a witch. Bradbury produced a petition signed by one hundred people who assured the judges she was innocent. This was ignored, but Bradbury eventually escaped, probably by bribing her jailers.

Of the second set of witches, Samuel Wardwell had a reputation for fortune-telling and confessed that he was "in the snare of the devil."[64] Abigail Falkner was saved from death because she was pregnant with an innocent life. Ann Forester was granted a reprieve for confessing to witchcraft but later died in prison. The eight people convicted in the last witch trial were hanged on September 22.

The End of the Witch Trials

After the last executions, the Court of Oyer and Terminer adjourned, expecting to meet later. But by October public opinion had turned. Increase Mather wrote a paper in which he questioned the court's tactics, and said it would be better for ten witches to go free than for one innocent person to be killed. On October 8, Thomas Brattle became the first powerful man to speak out against the madness. Brattle was one of Boston's most

educated men—he was a Harvard graduate, a world traveler, a mathematician, an astronomer, and a member of England's Royal Society.

In a letter reprinted in Calef's *More Wonders of the Invisible World,* Brattle suggested that the afflicted girls were deluded by the Devil, and the Devil's book, the witches' meetings, and the mock sacraments were figments of their imaginations. As for the confessors, some were known to be insane; others had been forced into false confessions.

Sir William Phipps returned from the frontier and found his court had failed to solve the witchcraft problem. The jails were still full and new accusations were being made every day. In a new approach, Phipps ordered the Superior Court of Judicature to hold special sessions to try persons still in jail. The court adjourned in January 1693 and found the previous court procedures had been faulty for allowing spectral evidence.

Fifty-two people were put on trial, but this time spectral evidence was not allowed. Of this group only three were con-

Martha Corey is tried for witchcraft. She and her husband, Giles, were found guilty and sentenced to death.

Clearing the Jails

More than 150 jailed suspects were granted general pardons by Massachusetts governor William Phipps. But clearing the jails took time. The prisoners were not allowed their freedom until they had paid the jailers for their food and other expenses. They even had to pay the cost for making the manacles and iron chains that kept them bound to the walls twenty-four hours a day.

Most of the alleged witches came from poor circumstances. Their families had great difficulty raising the money for their release. Some never recovered from the financial strain incurred in this effort. One woman was released only when she agreed to become the indentured servant of the man who had paid her debt. The property of the accused that had been confiscated by the sheriff was never returned, and a great number of the innocent lived out the rest of their lives in poverty.

victed. All were confessors and all were sentenced to death. But when the king's attorney general questioned the evidence against the condemned, Phipps granted them a reprieve. Finally in May 1693, Phipps began to clear the jails of more than 150 alleged witches. He also granted pardons to all, including those who had fled the colony.

When it was over, the townspeople began to pick up the pieces and put their lives back together.

Chapter

6 The Hangman's Noose

Historians believe that those accused of witchcraft were hanged outside of Salem on the first large hill, known as Gallows Hill or Witches' Hill. Visitors today can find Gallows Hill by taking Boston Road north from Essex Street. Those who do pass one of the only homes still standing from that time. It belonged to a magistrate in the witch trials, Jonathan Corwin. The house is still known as the Witch House for its gables, dark wood, and sinister appearance along with its association with Corwin, the famous witch-hunter. It is possible that some of the accused witches were questioned there. And the condemned prisoners would have passed by the house on their last earthly journey up Gallows Hill.

No mercy was shown to the condemned as they made their trip to the noose. They were mocked by the afflicted girls and a huge crowd who walked and ran alongside the cart carrying the chained prisoners. Some prisoners wept, some prayed silently. Those too weak to stand slumped on the floor of the cart. Those with the strength stood upright, gazing for the last time at the fields, trees, and rivers of the world they were about to leave.

The condemned might have also imagined in horror the world they believed they were going to. Since almost all of them were devout Christians, they must have given quite a great deal of thought to the torments of hell that awaited them. "Oh, hell is a terrible place, that's worse a thousand times than whipping,"[65] Cotton Mather had written.

Once the cart halted at the foot of the old oak or locust tree used for hanging, the prisoners were forced to walk up the last, steepest part of the hill. The jeers and insults of the crowd increased even as the condemned took their last steps. The

The Witch House in Salem (pictured) belonged to one of the magistrates in the trials, Jonathan Corwin.

mockery continued even as the men and women climbed—or were carried—up the ladder leaning against the highest branch of the tree where the nooses dangled.

Captain Nathaniel Cary, whose own wife had barely escaped the ordeal, wrote about the jeering crowd in a letter accusing the afflicted, the magistrates, and the ministers of acting in bad faith. Cary wrote:

> But to speak of their usage of the Prisoners, and the Inhumanity shewn to them, at the time of their Execution, no sober Christian could bear; they had also tryals of cruel mockings; which is the more, considering what a People of Religion, I mean the profession of it, we have been; those that suffered, many of them being Church-Members, and most of them unspotted in their Conversation, till their Adversary the Devil took up this Method of accusing them.[66]

But this "tryal of cruel mocking," as Cary described it, served a purpose for authorities. Most of the prisoners, believing their own innocence, carried themselves with dignity and grace right to the end. Some exclaimed their innocence with their last breath. The calm demeanor of the condemned would likely have raised doubts about their guilt among members of the crowd. The afflicted girls, their friends, and those actively engaged in the witch-hunt led the loud mocking to keep the hatred and hysteria at a fever pitch.

Once the prisoner climbed up the ladder, the executioner lowered the noose over his or her head and pulled it tightly around the person's neck. He then pushed the prisoner off the ladder to fall downward and swing sideways. After that, the executioner climbed down the ladder and removed it. Unless the prisoner managed to jump upward while being pushed to make the drop break his or her neck, death came by slow strangulation.

Hanging the Accused

On June 10, 1692, at eight o'clock in the morning, Bridget Bishop—the first person convicted of witchcraft—was taken from Salem prison. She was put in a cart and carried to Gallows Hill. Bishop was taken to the summit of the hill and hanged from a branch in an old oak tree. Her body was buried nearby, in a crevice in the sheer drop on one side of the hill. Bishop's passing seemed to have made little impression. There is no written account of the first hanging of an accused witch.

The second executions on July 19 must have been a much larger event, as five women were hanged that day. They were Sarah Good, Rebecca Nurse, Susannah Martin, Elizabeth Howe, and Sarah Wild. Nurse went to her death as she lived her life—as a good Christian with a forgiving heart. Given the fact that so many signed a petition in her favor, and that she was first found not guilty, her death must have caused many in the crowd to question the process. As Nurse stood on the ladder, she prayed to God—as did all the accused—to give some miraculous sign of her innocence. She also asked God to forgive those who had wronged her. The other women went the same way, showing resolve and praying for their accusers.

Two men prepare to hang Bridget Bishop on Gallows Hill. She was the first person to be convicted of witchcraft.

But of the batch of alleged witches hanged that day, there was one who was unable to show forgiveness. Sarah Good, at the foot of the hanging tree, was continually bullied by Reverend Nicholas Noyes to confess. The reverend announced to the crowd that Good was a witch and she knew it. Good's reply became famous and is remembered more than three hundred years later: "You are a liar," she told him, "I am no more a witch than you are a wizard, and if you must take my life God will give you blood to drink."[67]

This must have sent a chill through the crowd—only a witch—or a spiteful old woman—would die with a curse upon her lips. This curse was remembered twenty-five years later when Noyes lay dying. Tradition has it that he did indeed choke to death from internal bleeding.

Once all five women were dead, they were cut down from the hanging tree and their bodies were tossed into crevices in the rocks on the side of the hill. This saved the labor of digging a grave. No prayers were said, no respects given. Indeed, they were treated with the same hatred that they were shown in life.

For the relatives, such an end for their loved ones must have been exceedingly painful. The night after the hangings, young men of the Nurse family climbed up Gallows Hill under the cover of darkness and retrieved their grandmother's body. They brought her home and buried her, probably saying prayers in defiance of their church. Today there is a memorial to Rebecca Nurse in the family graveyard a few hundred feet down the hill from her former home.

The Hangings Continue

The second set of hangings took place on August 19, 1692. That day saw the death of George Burroughs, John Proctor, John Willard, the elderly George Jacobs, and Martha Carrier. Judge Samuel Sewall wrote that "all of them said they were innocent, Carrier and all."[68] Thomas Brattle, who was disgusted by the entire witch hysteria, wrote a letter that described the second wave of executions:

> Some of the condemned went out of the world not only with as great protestations, but also with as good shews of innocency, as men could do.

> They protested their innocency as in the presence of the great God, whom forthwith they were to appear before: they wished, and declared their wish, that their blood might be the last innocent blood shed upon that account. With great affection they intreated Mr. C[otton] M[ather] to pray with them: they prayed that God would discover what witchcrafts were among us; they forgave their accusers; they spake without reflection on Jury and Judges, for bringing them in guilty, and condemning them: they prayed earnestly for pardon for all other sins, and for an interest in the pretious blood of our dear Redeemer; and seemed to be very sincere, upright, and sensible of their circumstances on all accounts; especially Proctor and Willard, whose whole management of themselves, from the Gaol [jail] to the Gallows, and whilst at the Gallows, was very affecting and melting to the hearts of some considerable Spectatours.[69]

George Burroughs perhaps died the most dramatic death. Robert Calef wrote about it in *More Wonders of the Invisible World:*

> When [Burroughs] was upon the Ladder, he made a Speech for the clearing of his Innocency, with such Solemn and Serious Expressions, as were to the Admiration of all present; his Prayer (which he concluded by repeating the Lord's Prayer,) was so well worded, and uttered with such composedness, and such (at least seeming) fervency of Spirit, as was very affecting, and drew Tears from many (so that it seemed to some, that the Spectators would hinder the Execution).

Ending his prayer by repeating the Lord's Prayer was a brilliant move on the part of the condemned man. Popular belief held that a witch could not say the Lord's Prayer properly—the prayer was thought to be said backward at witches' Sabbaths. Suspects were often prodded to say the Lord's Prayer in court, a test they often failed because of nervousness and fear. Burroughs risked saying the prayer because if he would have stammered, or even stopped to swallow, the throng would have assumed he was guilty. But according to Calef, he got through to the crowd—so much so that Cotton Mather felt it necessary to reassure those gathered for the hangings. Calef continues:

> As [Burroughs] was turned off (killed), Mr. Cotton Mather, being mounted upon a Horse, addressed himself to the People, partly to declare, that [Burroughs] was no ordained Minister, and partly to possess the People of his guilt; saying, That the Devil has often been transformed into an Angel of Light and

George Burroughs (kneeling) recites the Lord's Prayer before being executed. His "fervency of Spirit" caused many in the crowd to doubt his guilt.

this did somewhat appease the People, and the Executions went on.[70]

The execution of George Burroughs produced the loudest outcry from the public and the most substantial belief in his innocence. Calef includes a note from judge Samuel Sewall's diary that reads

> Mr. Burroughs by his Speech, Prayer, and protestations of his Innocence, did much [to] move unthinking persons, which occasions their speaking hardly concerning his being executed.

In the margins he later added "Dolefull Witchcraft!"[71]

Of the others, George Jacobs Sr. perhaps said it best when he yelled to the crowd: "Well! Burn me or hang me, I will stand in the truth of Christ."[72]

The Death of Giles Corey

Perhaps the most shocking event of the witch madness took place about a month after Burroughs and the others were hanged. Giles Corey, who had testified against his wife, Martha, in March, was himself arrested. Giles, known for his stubbornness and eccentricities, refused to answer the questions of the magistrates. Corey said that he was innocent but if he went to trial, the same witnesses would be brought against him and he was

The Ballad of Giles Corey

When Giles Corey was pressed to death, rumor has it that his only words were "More weight, more weight." So famous was Corey's pressing that a ballad was written about it in the nineteenth century. It was reprinted in *A Delusion of Satan,* by Frances Hill.

Giles Cory was a wizard strong,
A stubborn wretch was he,
And fit was he to hang on high
Upon the locust tree.

So when before the magistrates
For trial he did come,
He would no true confession make
But was completely dumb.

"Giles Cory," said the magistrate,
"What have thou here to plead
To these who now accuse thy soul
of crimes and horrid deed?"

Giles Cory—he said not a word,
No single word spoke he.
"Giles Cory," said the magistrate,
"We'll press it out of thee."

They got them then a heavy beam,
They laid it on his breast.
They loaded it with heavy stones,
And hard upon him pressed.

"More weight," now said this wretched man,
"More weight," again he cried,
And he did no confession make
But wickedly he died.

Dame Cory lived but three days more,
But three days more lived she,
For she was hanged at Gallows Hill
Upon the locust tree.

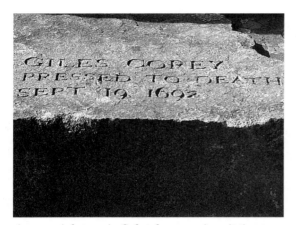

A memorial stone in Salem bears an inscription to Giles Corey. He was the only suspect to be pressed to death.

bound to be found guilty. He pointed out that the Court of Oyer and Terminer had never let anyone off. Corey said he "rather chose to undergo what death they would put him to."[73]

Corey possibly had another motive for not cooperating. If he was found legally guilty, his property could be confiscated. If he was not put to trial, his lands would remain in control of his heirs.

Whatever his motives, when Corey was taken to court with his wife on September 9, and with Ann Foster on September 17, he refused to speak. This incurred the wrath of the judges, who ordered Corey to be taken to an open field near the courthouse. Corey was made to lie on the ground while rocks were piled on his chest. This procedure was an old English method of extracting confessions. The weight of the rocks was supposed to force the word *guilty* or *innocent* out of the victim. It probably took Corey hours to die. His ribs finally cracked under the tons of rocks and his final breath was squeezed from his lungs.

Corey's death had an unsettling effect upon the populace. It was the first (and last) time pressing had been practiced in New England. Thomas Putnam feared Corey's gruesome death would set off a new round of opposition to the witch-hunt. To quell any protests, Putnam dashed off a letter to Judge Samuel Sewall. The letter was quoted in Cotton Mather's *The Wonders of the Invisible World*. It read as follows:

> The Last Night my Daughter Ann was grievously Tormented by Witches, Threatening that she should be Pressed to Death, before Giles Cory. But thro' the Goodness of a Gracious God, she had at last a little Respite. Whereupon there appeared unto her (she said) a man in a Winding Sheet, who told her Giles Cory had Murdered him by Pressing him to Death with his Feet. . . . The Apparition said, God Hardened [Corey's] Heart, that he should not hearken to the Advice of the Court and so Dy an easy Death; because, as it said, "It must be done to him as he has done to me."[74]

Putnam's letter deals with a rumor that Corey had killed a servant seventeen years earlier. It implies that the apparition seen by Ann was that of the allegedly murdered man. The letter was meant to show the judges that since Corey had supposedly murdered the man by pressing, Corey should receive the same punishment. It seems hard to believe, as Putnam writes, that Ann could have known about this incident, which happened before she was born. Perhaps the vision was really of her father's making.

The last hangings of those convicted of witchcraft took place on September 22,

1692. Those condemned to die were Martha Corey, Mary Easty, Alice Parker, Mary Parker, Ann Pudeater, Margaret Scott, Wilmot Redd, and Samuel Wardwell. This time the prison cart was weighted down with seven women and one man—its heaviest load yet. In fact it was said that the cart became mired in the mud and sank up to its axles while going up Gallows Hill. Calef writes in *More Wonders,* "The Cart going up the Hill with these Eight to Execution, was for some time at a sett; the afflicted and others said, that the Devil hindered it."[75]

"No More Innocent Blood Be Shed"

Mary Easty was accused of witchcraft and jailed April 21, 1692. She was released on May 18, however. Authorities believed Easty—a respected member of the community—when she claimed that the afflicted girls had cleared her name. But the afflicted girls did not clear Easty, and they had unusually violent fits when the suspected witch was freed. Easty was arrested again two days later. Before her execution Easty wrote a thoughtful letter to the judges who had condemned her. Thomas Calef reprinted it in *More Wonders,* and an excerpt follows:

> Your poor and humble Petitioner knowing my own Innocency (blessed be the Lord for it) . . . [sees] plainly the Wiles and Subtilty of my Accusers. . . . I Petition to your Honours not for my own Life, for I know I must die . . . [but] if it be possible, that no more Innocent Blood be shed, which un-doubtedly cannot be avoided in the way and course you go in. . . . I would humbly beg of you, that your Honours would be pleased to Examine some of those confessing Witches, I being confident there are several of them have belyed themselves and others, as will appear, if not in this World, I am sure in the World to come. . . . They say, my self and others have made a league with the Devil, we cannot confess. I know and the Lord he knows (as will shortly appear) they belye me, and so I question not, but they do others; the Lord alone, who is the searcher of all hearts, knows. . . . I beg your Honours not to deny this my humble Petition, from a poor dying Innocent person.

Calef goes on to describe the executions: "Martha Cory, Wife to Giles Cory, protesting her Innocency, concluded her Life with an Eminent Prayer upon the Ladder."

Wardwell's protest of his innocence was cut short by smoke from the executioner's pipe, which blew in his face and made him sputter and cough. Calef writes:

The Salem Witch-Hunt Death Toll

Persons Hanged for Witchcraft in 1692:

June 10—Bridget Bishop
July 19—Sarah Good
July 19—Elizabeth Howe
July 19—Susannah Martin
July 19—Rebecca Nurse
July 19—Sarah Wild
August 19—George Burroughs
August 19—Martha Carrier
August 19—George Jacobs
August 19—John Proctor
August 19—John Willard
September 19—Giles Corey (pressed to death)
September 22—Martha Corey
September 22—Mary Easty
September 22—Alice Parker
September 22—Mary Parker
September 22—Ann Pudeater
September 22—Margaret Scott
September 22—Wilmot Redd
September 22—Samuel Wardwell

Persons Accused of Witchcraft Who Died in Jail:
May 10, 1692—Sarah Osburn
June 16, 1692—Roger Toothaker
December 3, 1692—Ann Foster
March 10, 1693—Lydia Dustin

An unnamed infant of Sarah Good died with Good in jail prior to Good's hanging on July 19.

[Wardwell] At Execution while he was speaking to the People, protesting his Innocency, the Executioner being at the same time smoaking Tobacco, the smoak coming in [Wardwell's] Face, interrupted the Discourse, those Accusers said, the Devil hindered him with smoak.

Mary Easty, Sister also to Rebecka Nurse, when she took her last farewell of her Husband, Children, and Friends, was, as is reported by them present, as Serious, Religious, Distinct, and Affectionate as could well be exprest, drawing Tears from the Eyes of almost all present.

When the executioner's grisly task was completed, once again the ardent reverend Nicholas Noyes had his say. According to Calef:

After Execution Mr. Noyes turning . . . to the Bodies, said, what a sad thing it is to see Eight Firebrands of Hell hanging there.[76]

But those in the crowd, whose sympathies were stirred by the farewells of Mary Easty, probably doubted that any of the hanged were "Firebrands of Hell." Noyes's words may have had the opposite effect, igniting opposition to the hanging.

The September 22 executions were a turning point in the witch hysteria. The speeches made by Mary Easty, Martha Corey, and others must have aroused great sympathy with the assembled crowd. Their deep feelings of innocence, their last prayers, and their sad good-byes to their families could not have helped but invoke pity. Such feelings, combined with other developments, were to make these hangings the last.

The End of the Hysteria

By October 1692, 19 people had been executed, 1 man pressed to death, 150 people languished in prison, and about 200 more stood accused of witchcraft. While this hysteria continued, the voices of madness grew louder.

Abigail Williams had once claimed to have seen forty witches. But on August 25, an accused witch, Susannah Post, claimed to have attended a meeting with two hundred witches and then said she heard of "five hundred witches in the country." Mary Toothaker, another accused, put the number at 305 but said she heard witches discuss "pulling down the Kingdom of Christ and setting up the Kingdom of Satan." William Barker of Andover claimed he was at a witches' meeting where he heard "Satan's desire was to set up his own worship (in Salem Village), abolish all the churches in the land, and fall next upon Salem [Town] and so go through the country."[77]

The insanity was fueled by Reverend Parris. Every Sunday his sermons thundered that there were "multitudes" of witches in New England. But Parris's desperate attempt to turn back the tide of logic proved futile.

As September turned to October 1692 more and more voices of reason and dissent were heard above the witch hysteria. In a way, it was the afflicted girls who hastened the process. They went beyond all bounds when they began to accuse the richest and most powerful people in Massachusetts of witchcraft. Believing they were invulnerable, the girls claimed that the mother-in-law of magistrate John Corwin was a witch. They also named two sons of Simon Bradstreet, a distinguished former governor, along with the wife of Reverend John Hale of Beverly. Even more reckless was the "crying out" of the name of Lady Phipps, wife of Sir William—the governor. To quote Frances Hill in *A Delusion of Satan:*

> In their frenzy of gratified, murderous vengefulness they had come to think themselves mightier than the mightiest. They were quickly proved wrong. None of these powerful people was arrested, and a huge backlash ended the witch-hunt.[78]

On October 12, Governor Phipps wrote to the governing body in London to say that he had forbidden further imprisonment for witchcraft. On October 26, the General Court of Massachusetts voted for a day of fasting and a meeting of ministers to consider how to proceed "as to the witchcrafts."[79] On October 29, Sir William formally dismissed the Court of Oyer and Terminer.

An outburst flares at a witch trial during the height of the hysteria. During the fall of 1692, the madness began to wane as voices of reason and dissent took hold.

In November the afflicted girls were called to Gloucester when a soldier believed his ailing sister was bewitched. On the way to the examination, the girls were crossing Ipswich Bridge when they met an old woman. The girls fell into fits, but instead of turning on the accused witch, the passersby simply hurried past. The girls had lost their credibility and made no more accusations.

Setting the Accused Free

As weeks and months dragged on, 152 people languished in chains in the New England dungeon. Meanwhile, the General Court was busy installing the new charter that Increase Mather had brought to the colony in May. At least four of the judges on the General Court had served on the Court of Oyer and Terminer—no disgrace had fallen on the magistrates.

Thirty of the accused finally appeared before a special court on January 3, 1693. Twenty-seven of these cases were dismissed, with only three found guilty. The deputy governor signed a warrant for their speedy execution, along with five others who had been condemned by the Court of Oyer and Terminer, but, as Phipps wrote, "considering how the matter had been managed I sent a reprieve whereby the execution was stopped."[80]

After that, Williams wrote:

> There were at least fifty persons in prison in great misery by reason of the extream cold and their poverty. . . . I caused some of them to be lett out upon bayle and put the Judges upon considering of a way to reliefe others and prevent them from perishing in prison.[81]

Phipps then goes on to censure the entire affair and says he put a stop to

> the blak cloud that threatened this Province with destruccion; for whereas this delusion of the Devill did spread and its dismall effects touched the lives and estates of many of their Majesty's Subjects and the reputacion of some of the principall persons here, and indeed unhappily clogged and interrupted their Majesty's affaires which hath been a great vexation to me.[82]

Paying the Price of Innocence

The troubles did not end for many of the accused. Some had to stay behind bars because they could not pay their prison fees. Many were ruined physically and financially. Not only were they left owing money to the jailers, but their household goods and farm animals had been seized by the sheriff.

Prisoners were made to pay for what was called maintenance—fuel, clothes, transportation to and from jail, and court and general prison fees. They were even forced to pay for every paper drawn up relating to their cases, including the ones that discharged them from prison or reprieved their executions.

After the amnesty, the released prisoners began to petition the government of Massachusetts Bay Colony for restitution. They also wanted their records wiped clean, as they were still thought of as witches by many. Nothing was done in response.

In 1702, the General Court was presented with a petition asking for formal pardons for all the people who had been convicted, including those who had been hanged. The Massachusetts House of Representatives responded by passing a bill forbidding the use of spectral evidence in the future, and declaring that "the infamy and reproach cast on the names and posterity" of those found guilty should "in some measure be rolled away."[83] This resolution scarcely met the needs of the petitioners.

For almost ten years, the petitions continued, but no seized goods were returned and no restitution was granted. At last, in October 1710, the General Court passed an act reversing the convictions of those who were hanged. On December 17, 1711, the sum of 578 pounds and 12 shillings was granted to the petitioning relatives. The largest amount, 150 pounds, went to the Proctors, since John Proctor was the wealthiest person hanged. The heirs of George Jacobs Sr. got 50 pounds, as did the heirs of George Burroughs.

The rest of the monetary allotments seemed arbitrary. The relatives of the prosperous Elizabeth Howe, for example, received only twelve pounds, whereas the derelict husband of Sarah Good—who ac-

Suspected witches await their fate in prison. Many continued to suffer hardships such as poverty and sickliness after their cases were dismissed.

cused his own wife of witchcraft—got thirty pounds. Together, the families of only twenty-four who were executed, imprisoned, or died ended up with any compensation.

Several other wrongs were eventually righted. In 1703, Joseph Green, Salem Village's new minister, reversed the excommunication of Martha Corey. In 1712, the excommunications of Giles Corey and Rebecca Nurse were overturned. In 1697, Judge Samuel Sewall, fearing retribution from God, handed in a paper to the General Court saying he desired to take "the blame and shame" for his actions on the Court of Oyer and Terminer.

The Reverend Parris did admit to being wrong for his role in the trials. For two years, the relatives of those he helped condemn made his life miserable: They fought with him over issues of pay, his title to the parsonage, and his fitness for the job. In

September 1697, Parris finally quit his post in Salem Village. But his luck did not run out. He married a woman with money, and he was kept from poverty as he worked in a checkered career as a shopkeeper, schoolmaster, farmer, and property speculator. Parris died in 1720, leaving many debts that had to be paid by his children.

The girls who were the accusers seem to have escaped unscathed. Elizabeth Parris eventually married, as did Elizabeth Booth, Sarah Churchill, and Mary Walcott. Mercy Lewis also married, but only after having a baby out of wedlock. No one knows what became of Abigail Williams, Elizabeth Hubbard, Susannah Sheldon, or Mary Warren. Rumor has it that Williams never recovered but was "followed with diabolical molestations to her death."[84] (It is possible that Williams suffered some sort of undiagnosed mental disorder.)

In all, there was little remorse shown by the villagers over the great injustices committed against so many people. The Putnams, who were the most vociferous in the accusations, both died in 1699. Thomas was forty-six, his wife thirty-seven. Their daughter Ann survived, along with her nine siblings, but Ann, like her mother, died at the age of thirty-seven.

Zealous accusers such as Stoughton, Noyes, and Corey never expressed any regrets; in fact, they stood by their actions. The men went on to become successful merchants and politicians and lived to ripe old ages. Corey was buried in the oldest ceme-tery in Salem, his bones near to those of the relatives of people he imprisoned. Ironi-cally, Corey's bones also lie near the memor-ial that was erected three hundred years later to those who were executed. The memorial consists of twenty stones, each bearing the name of one who was executed during the year of Salem witch madness.

Witch-Hunts Today

Today there are women and men who practice a form of witchcraft known as

Judge Samuel Sewall reads from the paper in which he took full "blame and shame" for his actions during the trials.

The witch trials memorial at Salem. Each stone is inscribed with the name of a victim.

Wicca. They practice ancient magic rituals and worship a deity known as the Goddess, whom they believe to be the supreme spiritual ruler. Modern witches say their religion has nothing to do with Satan, since Wicca existed long before anyone conceived the idea of the Devil. They say contemporary witchcraft reveres nature and their magic is used to bring harmony, not harm, to the world.

The term *witch-hunt* is used in modern times to describe any official investigation carried out to uncover alleged subversive activities but actually used to harass those with differing viewpoints. The most famous American witch-hunt in recent memory took place in the 1950s during the so-called McCarthy Era. At that time thousands of Americans were hauled before a Senate committee run by Joseph McCarthy and questioned—in violation of their constitutional rights—about their political beliefs. Those who had been socialists or attended meetings with Communists at an earlier time had their lives and careers ruined. Some went to prison when they refused to answer probing questions about their political or religious beliefs.

It seems as long as great masses of people allow themselves to be whipped into hysteria by those with their own political agenda, the witch-hunts will continue. The only defenses against modern witch-hunts are education and tolerance for those of differing beliefs.

Notes

Introduction: From Goddess to Evil

1. Quoted in Editors of Time-Life Books, *Witches and Witchcraft*. Alexandria, VA: Time-Life Books, 1990, p. 11.

2. Quoted in Editors of Time-Life Books, *Witches and Witchcraft*, p. 25.

3. Quoted in Editors of Time-Life Books, *Witches and Witchcraft*, p. 64.

Chapter 1: Puritan Life in Salem

4. Frances Hill, *A Delusion of Satan*. New York: Doubleday, 1995, p. 10.

5. Nathaniel Hawthorne, *Novels*. New York: Literary Classics of the United States, 1983, p. 198.

6. Quoted in Frances Hill, *A Delusion of Satan*, p. 11.

Chapter 2: Madness Comes to Salem

7. Quoted in Chadwick Hansen, *Witchcraft at Salem*. New York: George Braziller, 1969, p. 12.

8. Quoted in Chadwick Hansen, *Witchcraft at Salem*, p. 13.

9. Reprinted in George Lincoln Burr, ed., *Narratives of the Witchcraft Cases 1648–1706*. New York: Charles Scribner's Sons, 1914; reprinted, New York: Barnes & Noble, 1975, pp. 18–21.

10. Reprinted in George Lincoln Burr, ed., *Narratives of the Witchcraft Cases 1648–1706*, pp. 101–102.

11. Reprinted in George Lincoln Burr, ed., *Narratives of the Witchcraft Cases 1648–1706*, p. 100.

12. Reprinted in George Lincoln Burr, ed., *Narratives of the Witchcraft Cases 1648–1706*, p. 154.

13. Reprinted in George Lincoln Burr, ed., *Narratives of the Witchcraft Cases 1648–1706*, p. 162.

14. Quoted in Chadwick Hansen, *Witchcraft at Salem*, p. 2.

15. Quoted in Chadwick Hansen, *Witchcraft at Salem*, p. 33.

16. Quoted in Charles W. Upham, *Salem Witchcraft*, vol. 2. Williamstown, MA: Corner House, 1971 (first published 1867), p. 95.

Chapter 3: Making Accusations

17. Quoted in Chadwick Hansen, *Witchcraft at Salem*, p. 33.

18. Quoted in Chadwick Hansen, *Witchcraft at Salem*, p. 33.

19. Quoted in Chadwick Hansen, *Witchcraft at Salem*, p. 34.

20. Quoted in Chadwick Hansen, *Witchcraft at Salem*, p. 32.

21. Quoted in Chadwick Hansen, *Witchcraft at Salem*, p. 33.

22. Quoted in Alice Dickinson, *The Salem Witchcraft Delusion*. New York: Franklin Watts, 1974, p. 24.

23. Quoted in Chadwick Hansen, *Witchcraft at Salem*, p. 36.

24. Quoted in Charles W. Upham, *Salem Witchcraft*, vol. 2, p. 23–24.

25. Quoted in Charles W. Upham, *Salem Witchcraft*, vol. 2, p. 25.

26. Quoted in Chadwick Hansen, *Witchcraft at Salem*, p. 39.

27. Quoted in Chadwick Hansen, *Witchcraft at Salem*, p. 39.

Chapter 4: The Widening Circle

28. Quoted in Chadwick Hansen, *Witchcraft at Salem*, p. 40.

29. Reprinted in George Lincoln Burr, ed., *Narratives of the Witchcraft Cases 1648–1706*, p. 154.

30. Quoted in Chadwick Hansen, *Witchcraft at Salem,* p. 42.

31. Reprinted in George Lincoln Burr, ed., *Narratives of the Witchcraft Cases 1648–1706,* p. 156.

32. Reprinted in George Lincoln Burr, ed., *Narratives of the Witchcraft Cases 1648–1706,* pp. 155–56.

33. Reprinted in George Lincoln Burr, ed., *Narratives of the Witchcraft Cases 1648–1706,* p. 156.

34. Reprinted in George Lincoln Burr, ed., *Narratives of the Witchcraft Cases 1648–1706,* p. 156.

35. Quoted in Chadwick Hansen, *Witchcraft at Salem,* p. 51.

36. Reprinted in George Lincoln Burr, ed., *Narratives of the Witchcraft Cases 1648–1706,* p. 159.

37. Reprinted in George Lincoln Burr, ed., *Narratives of the Witchcraft Cases 1648–1706,* p. 160.

38. Quoted in Chadwick Hansen, *Witchcraft at Salem,* p. 52.

39. Quoted in Chadwick Hansen, *Witchcraft at Salem,* p. 55.

40. Reprinted in George Lincoln Burr, ed., *Narratives of the Witchcraft Cases 1648–1706,* p. 161.

41. Quoted in Alice Dickinson, *The Salem Witchcraft Delusion,* p. 36.

42. Reprinted in George Lincoln Burr, ed., *Narratives of the Witchcraft Cases 1648–1706,* p. 361.

43. Quoted in Alice Dickinson, *The Salem Witchcraft Delusion,* p. 37.

44. Quoted in Alice Dickinson, *The Salem Witchcraft Delusion,* p. 39.

45. Quoted in Alice Dickinson, *The Salem Witchcraft Delusion,* p. 40.

Chapter 5: The Witch Trials

46. Quoted in Frances Hill, *A Delusion of Satan,* p. 153.

47. Reprinted in George Lincoln Burr, ed., *Narratives of the Witchcraft Cases 1648–1706,* p. 196.

48. Reprinted in George Lincoln Burr, ed., *Narratives of the Witchcraft Cases 1648–1706,* p. 196.

49. Chadwick Hansen, *Witchcraft at Salem,* p. 122.

50. Quoted in Chadwick Hansen, *Witchcraft at Salem,* p. 65.

51. Quoted in Alice Dickinson, *The Salem Witchcraft Delusion,* p. 158.

52. Quoted in Chadwick Hansen, *Witchcraft at Salem,* p. 125.

53. Quoted in Frances Hill, *A Delusion of Satan,* p. 156.

54. Reprinted in George Lincoln Burr, ed., *Narratives of the Witchcraft Cases 1648–1706,* p. 358.

55. Reprinted in George Lincoln Burr, ed., *Narratives of the Witchcraft Cases 1648–1706,* p. 358.

56. Quoted in Charles W. Upham, *Salem Witchcraft,* vol. 2, p. 285.

57. Quoted in Charles W. Upham, *Salem Witchcraft,* vol. 2, p. 285.

58. Reprinted in George Lincoln Burr, ed., *Narratives of the Witchcraft Cases 1648–1706,* pp. 362–63.

59. Quoted in Frances Hill, *A Delusion of Satan,* p. 176.

60. Frances Hill, *A Delusion of Satan,* p. 177.

61. Reprinted in George Lincoln Burr, ed., *Narratives of the Witchcraft Cases 1648–1706,* p. 241.

62. Reprinted in George Lincoln Burr, ed., *Narratives of the Witchcraft Cases 1648–1706,* p. 244.

63. Reprinted in George Lincoln Burr, ed., *Narratives of the Witchcraft Cases 1648–1706,* pp. 366–67.

64. Frances Hill, *A Delusion of Satan,* p. 187.

Chapter 6: The Hangman's Noose

65. Quoted in Frances Hill, *A Delusion of Satan*, p. 11.

66. Reprinted in George Lincoln Burr, ed., *Narratives of the Witchcraft Cases 1648–1706*, p. 352.

67. Quoted in Chadwick Hansen, *Witchcraft at Salem*, p. 126.

68. Quoted in Chadwick Hansen, *Witchcraft at Salem*, p. 146.

69. Reprinted in George Lincoln Burr, ed., *Narratives of the Witchcraft Cases 1648–1706*, p. 177.

70. Reprinted in George Lincoln Burr, ed., *Narratives of the Witchcraft Cases 1648–1706*, pp. 360–61.

71. Reprinted in George Lincoln Burr, ed., *Narratives of the Witchcraft Cases 1648–1706*, p. 361.

72. Quoted in Frances Hill, *A Delusion of Satan*, p. 175.

73. Quoted in Frances Hill, *A Delusion of Satan*, p. 184.

74. Reprinted in George Lincoln Burr, ed., *Narratives of the Witchcraft Cases 1648–1706*, p. 250.

75. Reprinted in George Lincoln Burr, ed., *Narratives of the Witchcraft Cases 1648–1706*, p. 367.

76. Reprinted in George Lincoln Burr, ed., *Narratives of the Witchcraft Cases 1648–1706*, pp. 367–69.

Epilogue: The End of the Hysteria

77. Quoted in Frances Hill, *A Delusion of Satan*, p. 193.

78. Quoted in Frances Hill, *A Delusion of Satan*, p. 195.

79. Quoted in Frances Hill, *A Delusion of Satan*, p. 199.

80. Reprinted in George Lincoln Burr, ed., *Narratives of the Witchcraft Cases 1648–1706*, p. 201.

81. Reprinted in George Lincoln Burr, ed., *Narratives of the Witchcraft Cases 1648–1706*, p. 200.

82. Reprinted in George Lincoln Burr, ed., *Narratives of the Witchcraft Cases 1648–1706*, p. 201.

83. Quoted in Frances Hill, *A Delusion of Satan*, p. 205.

84. Quoted in Frances Hill, *A Delusion of Satan*, p. 215.

For Further Reading

George Lincoln Burr, ed., *Narratives of the Witchcraft Cases 1648–1706*. New York: Charles Scribner's Sons, 1914. Reprint, New York: Barnes & Noble, 1975. This old book contains some of the original court transcripts of the Salem witch trials along with letters and essays written at that time including the writings of Cotton and Increase Mather, Robert Calef, Deodat Lawson, and others. This book provides the original source quotes about the trials that have been used in dozens of other books.

Alice Dickinson, *The Salem Witchcraft Delusion*. New York: Franklin Watts, 1974. A book written for young adults about the Salem witch trials. Informative and easy to read.

Editors of Time-Life Books, *Witches and Witchcraft*. Alexandria, VA: Time-Life Books, 1990. A big, colorful book by Time-Life from the Mysteries of the Unknown series. Contains photos, ancient woodcuts, and old paintings of witches and witch trials. There is a long chapter on the European witch-hunts as well as several chapters covering female spirit worship from ancient Sumeria to modern Wicca.

Nathaniel Hawthorne, *Novels*. New York: Literary Classics of the United States, 1983. A book containing *The Scarlet Letter* and other novels of Nathaniel Hawthorne, great-great-grandson of the main witch inquisitor John Hathorne. Although the language is a little hard to read, Hawthorne is a scathing writer, often humorous, whose *Scarlet Letter* and *The House of the Seven Gables* are well worth reading.

Frances Hill, *A Delusion of Satan*. New York: Doubleday, 1995. One of the newest books written about the Salem madness, by an English author who uses modern psychology and feminism to question the forces behind the witch-hunts.

Stuart Kallen, *Witches, Magic, and Spells*. Minneapolis, MN: Abdo & Daughters, 1991. An easy-to-read book that details the history of witches and witchcraft from ancient times.

Wendy Stein, *Witches*. San Diego: Greenhaven Press, 1995. A great book for young adults from the Opposing Viewpoints series that presents both sides of the witchcraft debate from ancient times to modern Wicca.

Works Consulted

Paul Boyer and Stephen Nissenbaum, *Salem Possessed*. Cambridge, MA: Harvard University Press, 1974. An intricate and fascinating portrait of the politics behind the Salem witch hysteria. The authors show that many of the accusations were the result of divided families, farmers warring over land titles, and embittered children.

Chadwick Hansen, *Witchcraft at Salem*. New York: George Braziller, 1969. A thorough reading of the Salem witch hysteria by an author who believes witchcraft was actually practiced in Salem and some of those hanged were not innocent.

Carol F. Karlsen, *The Devil in the Shape of a Woman*. New York: W. W. Norton, 1987. A book that puts the Salem witch hysteria in perspective by delving into the structure of Puritan society and the relationships between men and women.

Marc Mappen, ed., *Witches and Historians*. Malabar, FL: Robert E. Krieger, 1980. A book that attempts to put the witch hysteria in perspective using works written by other authors. Includes writings by physicians who specialize in medical and psychological analysis as well as social historians and other intellectuals.

Arthur Miller, *Arthur Miller's Collected Plays*. New York: Viking, 1957. A book containing Miller's plays, including *The Crucible*, a fictionalized account of the Salem madness written during the McCarthy Era.

Jeffrey Burton Russell, *Witchcraft in the Middle Ages*. Ithaca, NY: Cornell University Press, 1972. A long account of the gruesome witch-hunts that wracked Europe in the Middle Ages.

Charles W. Upham, *Salem Witchcraft*. Vols. 1 and 2. Williamstown, MA: Corner House, 1971 (first published 1867). These two volumes contain more than nine hundred pages that study the Salem witch trials. The first volume, published in 1867, is a detailed history of Salem Village; the second covers the accusations, examinations, trials, and executions in vivid detail.

Index

Venus figurines, 10

Walcott, Mary, 35, 83
Wardwell, Samuel, 68, 77, 78–79
Warren, Mary, 35
    accused, 54
    examination of, 54–55
    after trials, 83
white magic, 11, 32, 51
Wicca, 84–85
Wild, Sarah, 62, 71
Willard, John, 66, 72
Willard, Samuel, 63
Williams, Abigail
    background of, 28, 29

fits of, 31–32
    after trials, 83
Winthrop, Wait, 59
witch cakes, 32
witchcraft
    criminal grounds for, 60, 61, 62
    goddesses and, 10–11
    present-day, 84–85
Witchcraft at Salem (Hansen), 36, 46–47, 48, 59
Witches and Witchcraft (editors of Time-Life Books), 11, 12, 40

Witches' Hammer (Kramer and Sprenger), 12–13
Witches' Hill, 70
Witch House, 70
witch's brooms, 43
witch's marks, 39, 40
women
    demonized, 13
    goddess worship and, 10–11
    Puritan, 37
Wonders of the Invisible World, The (Mather, Cotton), 66

Picture Credits

About the Author

Stuart A. Kallen is the author of more than 135 nonfiction books for children and young adults. He has written on topics ranging from the theory of relativity to rock-and-roll history to life on the American frontier. In addition, Mr. Kallen has written award-winning children's videos and television scripts. Mr. Kallen lives in San Diego, California.